MASTER
the *Genie*
WITHIN

Praise for Master the Genie Within

"Not only do I love the genie metaphor, but the practical advice made me look at the inner workings of my own thoughts in new and rewarding ways."

— Tyler R. Tichelaar, Ph.D.
and author of the award-winning *Narrow Lives*

"Engaging and informative... speaks to you and explains how we, as women, are taught from an early age to take on social roles and labels based on what our culture and society expects of us. *Master the Genie Within* also gives you tools to help you step out of those roles and labels to become your true authentic self you were destined to be."

— Michele Broadnax

"Drawing on her experience as a marriage and family therapist, Gladys Anderson has created a self-discovery guide that brings a fresh perspective to uncovering our authentic selves. Chock full of practical and actionable steps, this book is the perfect companion for anyone ready to experience increased happiness and fulfillment."

— Flora Morris Brown, Ph.D.
and author of *Color Your Life Happy*

"*Master the Genie Within* takes you on a journey of authentic self-discovery that creates an even greater awareness of how you think, feel, and respond to the world...a thorough and engaging read."

— Katrina Chesney,
Portable Hands

"*Master the Genie Within* is a much needed work for our time. It not only tells us, but shows us how to tap into our inner environment. In tapping into our Inner Genie we can create the life we desire, instead of one created for us."

— Penelope Jackson Bowie, Spiritual Life Coach

"Powerful, graceful and real! *Master the Genie Within* identifies the masks that we wore as well as the steps we need to take to become the ideal person we were meant to be."

— Carolyn Guilford

"*Master the Genie Within: Uncover, Embrace and Celebrate the Real You* is an enlightening guide on the rewards of living a fearless, joyful, and authentic life - the life we are meant to live."

— Maria Pacheco, LCSW

"*Master the Genie Within* is what I've been searching for all these years! I finally have a better understanding of how I've been feeling, reacting and responding to others. This book has helped me to master my own personal genie."

— Susan Robertson

MASTER
the
Genie
WITHIN

UNCOVER, EMBRACE AND CELEBRATE THE REAL YOU

Gladys M. Anderson, LMFT, CTACC

Published by Nia Publishers
Hartford, CT

ISBN: 978-0-9854249-0-9

Disclaimer:
The names and stories in this book have been modified
to protect client confidentiality. The stories are fictional-
ized examples, combining multiple real-life client
experiences to create a fictional client whose story will
illustrate the scenarios and points being discussed. None
of the stories reflect direct biographical material of an
individual real-life client.

This book is dedicated to the memory of my mother, Mrs. Dorothy M. Pinnix

*The purpose of life is to
live it, to taste experience
to the utmost, to reach
out eagerly and without
fear for newer and richer
experience.*

— Eleanor Roosevelt

Acknowledgments

With deep appreciation, I am grateful to a number of people for their support, encouragement, skills, and talents.

I am forever grateful to all the women writers, mothers, sisters, daughters, grandmothers, and aunts on whose shoulders I stand.

An abiding appreciation goes to my husband, Wilfred Anderson, Jr., who continuously provides me with unyielding support, and who gives me space to be creative and the freedom to explore my many pursuits.

I feel gratitude for my wise beyond her years daughter, Cheryl Coleman, my biggest cheerleader, who has never wavered in her support of my writing and helps me to see the big picture.

Many thanks to my friend, mentor, and colleague, Dr. Flora M. Brown, who has provided me with inspiration and sustained me throughout the writing and publication processes.

Special appreciation goes to my editor, Tyler Tichelaar, who helped me weave all the pieces together to present a clear picture of my intent.

And, last but not least, I wish to thank my dearest friends [you know who you are] for their steadfast, love, support, and encouragement.

Table of Contents

Introduction 9

Chapter 1 Uncover Your True Self Behind the Mask ... 15

Chapter 2 Set Strong Boundaries to
Balance Your Life 39

Chapter 3 Invisible Woman No More 51

Chapter 4 An Attitude of Gratitude Attracts
More Abundance 57

Chapter 5 Exchanging Harmful Thoughts for
Helpful Habits 69

Chapter 6 Exposing Limiting Beliefs that Keep You
Stuck in Fear 77

Chapter 7 The Most Important Relationship You Will
Ever Have is With Yourself 81

Chapter 8 Creating Space for Quiet Time
and Reflection 109

Chapter 9 Simplify and Systematize Your Life 113

Chapter 10 You Are the Captain of Your Soul 121

Chapter 11 Give Without Giving Up Yourself 135

Chapter 12 Set Limits on Your Time and Energy 139

Chapter 13 Stop the Merry-go-Round!
   I Want to Get Off 149

Chapter 14 Communication Influences How Well
   You Are Perceived 159

Chapter 15 Celebrate You 173

   Afterword 179

   Recommended Reading 181

   About the Author 183

Introduction

Each of us has within us everything we need to live a happy, successful, and productive life. We can do, be, and have whatever we desire. All of our dreams, wishes, hopes, and desires are simply waiting for us once we learn how to tap into the power of manifestation—the ability to create with intention the life we want for ourselves.

This book will take you on a journey of self-discovery and self-growth. It will open your eyes to an even greater awareness of how you think, feel, and respond to the world.

How you navigate your world is a direct reflection of the messages you've internalized about how your life *should* be. Your thoughts, beliefs, fears, and expectations are directly connected to the hidden messages in your subconscious mind that influence your every decision, response, and reaction.

This dynamic is played out in your intimate relationships and also in how you interact with your family, friends, neighbors, and co-workers.

Until limiting beliefs and hidden messages are brought to the light of day, I doubt if you will find the strength, trust, and belief to focus on your own desires without guilt and frustration.

If you are reading this book, you probably realize something is holding you back in life, making you unhappy, or at the least, you are not experiencing the full happiness and sense of fulfillment you desire. Don't beat yourself up about this. You are not alone. We all have a tendency to hold ourselves back.

Congratulations! You are now ready to do something about it.

Once you learn what the hidden messages are that hold you back, and how to change those beliefs, you'll have mastered the genie within and you will be prepared to use your magic, metaphorically, to your advantage to manifest the life you desire.

In my work as a psychotherapist, I often encounter women who are struggling to find their voices. They struggle to stand up and take risks. They focus on the desires of others, ignoring what is right for them. They are like young seedlings with infinite possibilities waiting to germinate and burst forth in full bloom. My job is to help them find those voices, to unlock the power or genie within them.

Let me explain why I use the term "genie." We probably all know what genies are—those magical beings from Arabian myths and legends who tend to live in bottles or lamps, and who will grant us three wishes. A lot of genies, however, are mischievous and troublesome. They may have magic powers, but they don't always use them for good but to do harm. However, when someone owns the lamp or bottle the genie is in, that person has control over the genie. I'm going to use the genie idea as a metaphor for the power we all have within us. Our goal in this book will be to learn how to use that power to assist us, to empower us, rather than to harm ourselves or hold us back.

In the book *What Mama Couldn't Tell Us About Love*, authors Brenda Richardson and Brenda Wade discuss how a lot of the messages women receive are couched in fear and self-doubt. This begins at an early age when the messages they receive do not align with their spirits. For instance, it can occur when little girls are taught that sports are for boys while homemaking is for girls or that big boys don't cry.

I can remember when fear and doubt began to creep into my psyche. I was probably about six or seven when I first noticed that I was being told how dangerous life was, and systematically, I was taught to doubt my instincts and mistrust my decisions. I was constantly being told, "Don't do that," "Don't go there," and "Don't think or do that because it's dangerous," "You might get hurt," or "It's not good for you." These messages formed a foundation of fear and self-doubt inside me.

What a dangerous message to send an impressionable child, especially a little girl who will need all the reserves she can muster to overcome challenges and risk believing in herself!

In this book, we will explore the hidden patterns of self-doubt, roadblocks to change, and irrational beliefs. Once we identify those hidden patterns that hold us back, we will look for ways to replace them by inviting authenticity into our lives. The goal of this book is to focus on ways to change the flawed thinking that leads to poor choices, unfilled lives, mediocrity, and distrust.

I have taken this journey myself and not only discovered my genie within but learned how to master her. As a result, I've experienced the magic of much more than the usual three wishes. Now my wish is that you will join me in this journey so you can discover and know the power of your own genie!

Gladys Anderson

*Use the contact form at
www.coachforyourdreams.com
to ask any questions you have.
I'll respond promptly.*

List three wishes that you want your genie to fulfill:

1. _____

_____

_____

2. _____

_____

_____

3. _____

_____

_____

Your three wishes will be the inspiration and motivation to complete the exercises and use the tools in this book to uncover, embrace and celebrate the real you.

CHAPTER 1

Uncover Your True Self Behind the Mask

"We all have the extraordinary coded within us, waiting to be released."

— Jean Houston

As I said in the introduction, sometimes genies can be troublesome or tricksters—they can wear "masks" to deceive us about who they are. Our internal genie might disguise herself or her behaviors by pretending to do something for our good, perhaps simply under the guise of protecting us, when those thoughts or actions might really cause us harm. For example, we might decide not to participate in a group where we will have to speak in public—our genie tells us that not participating is a way to protect ourselves from ridicule—but in reality, public speaking can help us build self-esteem and courage. The mask of protection is just that—a mask that disguises fear as well as possibility.

Let's look at reasons why people wear masks. Ancient cultures used masks for a variety of reasons, including to ward off evil spirits and to connect with ancestors' spirits and other spiritual beings. The first known masks were the funerary masks created in Egypt. Funerary masks were thought to transition the physical presence from the world into an afterlife.

Webster's New World Dictionary defines a mask as "a protective covering worn to conceal, disguise, or hide one's true motives, character, or identity."

Today, most of us are accustomed to wearing masks at carnivals, festivals, and children's parties. Halloween is a familiar example of the power of pretense and the appeal of masks.

Given the historical relevance of masks, it's no wonder we can so readily adopt masks to hide who we really are.

There are times when wearing an emotional mask may be appropriate, such as wearing a mask to hide intimate details of our lives from the world. For example, parents may want to hide personal information from their children, such as details about their sex lives. Masks can be powerful tools to protect sensitive information, but can play havoc with your personal success when they become a permanent fixture in expressing your true self.

Often the mask is a survival tool we learn early in life. We use a mask to protect ourselves from pain, suffering, and emotional upheaval.

While you might not readily think of a smile as a mask, it is a type of mask. Scientists speculate that our ancestors gradually developed the smile nerves as a way to force smiles because they were a useful way to mask their fear and anger.

Paul Laurence Dunbar's poem, "*We Wear the Mask*" so accurately describes how the smile serves to mask our pain and suffering:

> *We wear the mask that grins and lies,*
> *It hides our cheeks and shades our eyes,—*
> *This debt we pay to human guile;*
> *With torn and bleeding hearts we smile,*
> *And mouth with myriad subtleties.*
>
> *Why should the world be over-wise,*
> *In counting all our tears and sighs?*
> *Nay, let them only see us, while*
> *   We wear the mask.*
>
> *We smile, but, O great Christ, our cries*
> *To thee from tortured souls arise.*
> *We sing, but oh the clay is vile*
> *Beneath our feet, and long the mile;*
> *But let the world dream otherwise,*
> *   We wear the mask!*

Dunbar was the son of slaves. And, although his poem does not specifically mention slavery, more than likely his parents' experiences as slaves influenced this poem considerably. His poem speaks a universal language to anyone who hides behind a mask to avoid revealing his or her true feelings.

Let's look at a classic example of how a person today hides behind a mask. We'll call this person "Margie." Margie thinks she has to fix everything for everyone in her life. She's the ultimate "Ms. Fix-It," who often goes out of her way to make sure everyone is okay, often anticipating others' needs before they express them. She's the go-between in every family conflict, every disagreement among friends, and is frequently the one who apologizes quickly for some ill-conceived wrongdoing. Even when Margie is angry, sad, hurt, or disappointed and wants to scream, she dons a smile and puts on a happy face.

Margie tries to make things better by attempting to control her surroundings and restoring some harmony to her disorganized life. Although Margie knows on a conscious level that her behaviors are uncomfortable and unhealthy, she is at a loss regarding what she can do to change. And, as a result, she wears the role of Ms. Fix-It like a comfortable old shoe and carries this pattern of behavior into every relationship.

Sadly, Margie is not alone. Countless people fall prey to these same scenarios repeatedly in their relationships. And it's not their fault. Cultural, societal, and family patterns are usually at the root of this kind of behavior. Those patterns make us behave the way we think, subconsciously or consciously, other people want us to behave.

Let me give you a simple example from my own life. I grew up in a small southern town with many role expectations and cultural traditions. One of those expectations was that women wear hats and gloves to church, and women do not wear pants. I didn't like hats because I have a small head and hats that fit me were hard to come by.

Nor did I see any good reason why I shouldn't wear pants if I wanted to. But to "fit in" and be viewed as a "lady," I conformed and slipped on a false mask of womanhood until I learned that I didn't have to conform to be accepted. To this day, I only wear hats if I choose to and pants are a staple of my wardrobe.

Anytime you take on roles that are uncomfortable and not of your own choosing, you are wearing a mask that can start a lifetime of personal deception.

Unsatisfying patterns of behavior, struggling to maintain relationships, or confusion about some of the reactions and responses you have are probably an indication that you're wearing a mask. And, unconsciously, the mask becomes a badge of protection that gets your emotional needs met.

Disguises We Use to Protect Ourselves

One of the main reasons for wearing a mask is to pretend to be someone or something else. Below we'll look at some of the people we pretend to be when we wear a mask.

The Champion: The Champion defends and makes excuses for everyone and everything often to her own peril. She is the self-designated cheerleader wherever she goes. She's the one who attempts to orchestrate the social and emotional climate in every interaction she has. But champions are not cheerleaders. These people are afraid to experience anything they perceive as negative. So they spend their lives putting on a "happy face" when inside they are angry and hurt, and they fear rejection and abandonment. Champions often make excuses for others' bad behavior and often blame themselves when "everybody can't just get along."

We wear the mask that grins and lies...it hides our cheeks and shades our eyes...

The Follower: The Follower is your typical "yes" woman. She agrees to do things that make her skin crawl, but she doesn't have the courage to say, "No." More than likely, she learned this behavior early in life. As a child, the Follower grew up with the mistaken notion of, "If I do what I'm told, I'll be loved and accepted." Followers have a hard time **not** conforming and difficulty thinking outside of the box.

The Wounded: The Wounded is the super-sensitive one whose fragile feelings are easily hurt. She creates in her head a story that says, "I'm not good enough," or "Something is wrong with me" whenever she feels slighted, talked about, or ignored. And because she truly believes she's not good enough, the most innocent words or actions can send her into her self-imposed shell of withdrawal, hurt, and anger. When you witness this kind of response from a person, you are more than likely looking at someone with low self-worth.

Wonder Woman: The Wonder Woman, or Superwoman, concept has taken on its own meaning in songs, feminists groups, and various cultures. The original Wonder Woman first appeared in *All Star Comics* #8 (December 1941). She had superhuman strength and magical powers. She was highly proficient in hand-to-hand combat and in the art of tactical warfare.

You may not recall the comic book version, but most of us are familiar with the TV series *The New Adventures of Wonder Woman* starring Lynda Carter.

Today, when we use the term Wonder Woman or Superwoman, we think of someone who is able to take on herculean tasks without breaking a sweat. Only, because she thinks she has Wonder Woman's powers, it's like she's wearing a big sign on her forehead that says, "I'm available. Pick me!" She accepts even more commitments and responsibilities. And when the stress mounts, she beats herself up because she can't get it all done.

The People Pleaser: People pleasers often have poor boundaries around their time, energy, and resources. They want to make sure everyone is taken care of— no matter the price they may have to pay. When people pleasers feel their efforts are not appreciated, they develop an underlying and deep sense of overall unworthiness, and a buried desire to be validated. People pleasers just want everyone to be happy and get along. They usually do whatever is asked of them, and they worry how others will perceive them.

We were not born to be people pleasers. It's a learned response. Notice how demanding babies are? They're born that way. Babies have an uncanny ability of letting adults know what they want and when they want something. They cry when they need changing or want to eat, and they let you know loud and clear when they want attention. It never crosses their little minds to people-please!

We learn how to respond to the world through the lens of the adults who care for us and other important people in our lives. For example, if you grew up in a family where you witnessed your mother taking care of everyone but herself, it's more than likely you will enter adulthood believing your needs are not important and that others come first. Or adults may have sent you the message that, "Your feelings and thoughts are not important" so you were often discouraged from expressing how you felt.

The Heroine: This woman may have taken on the role of "parent" at an early age—cooking, cleaning, and taking care of younger siblings. She was a good student and showed unusual self-sufficiency. She was often seen as an overachiever. While she appears successful on the outside, on the inside she feels inadequate and insecure. She is unaware of her true feelings. A false show of responsibility may hide her real desire to have someone take care of her.

The Scapegoat: As a child, the Scapegoat often had behavior problems in school—getting into fights, skipping classes, or playing the role of class clown. Her antics more than likely were futile attempts to draw attention away from the internal turmoil caused by conflict and tension in her family. While all attention is on the "problem child," the family can avoid addressing the causal issues of anger, sibling rivalry, marital discord, alcoholism, and arguments. In adulthood, you may see a scapegoat as the person who can't seem to get along with peers; she often has disputes about trivial matters because she's uncomfortable in any situation she views as conflict and believes that she needs to act out as a diversion.

The Loner: The Loner is often the quiet, shy one in the family. She doesn't make waves and tries not to be a bother to anyone. She feels forgotten and different, often wondering whether she really belongs in the family. Loners go into adulthood with few close friends and tend to spend their time reading, watching television, or listening to music. They appear self-sufficient and independent, but they secretly wish for an active, involved, and rewarding life.

Ms. Fix-it: Ms. Fix-it is ever ready to step forward with a big smile to help amend, negotiate, or smooth over any disagreement or disturbance even when it's not of her own making. She can't bear the perception that someone is unhappy or in distress. She truly believes that she is responsible for everyone else's emotional state.

The Apologizer: The Apologizer is someone who over-apologizes, a trait that can usually be traced back to a woman's early family relationships. Women who grew up with disapproving parents, or experienced maltreatment, often apologize as a way to calm down others and avoid confrontation. There is nothing wrong with apologizing when you make a mistake, or hurt or disappoint someone. However, when you constantly apologize for trivial things that are not within the realm of your responsibility, it brings into question your sincerity and self-confidence.

A lot of women will say "I'm sorry" whenever they make even the smallest request such as asking for a small favor or just asking someone to speak louder so you can hear him.

To get past this tendency, it is important you become aware of how often you are apologizing and be clear about what you are apologizing for. For example, if you find you regularly say, "I'm sorry, do you have the time?" instead say, "What time do you have?"

Like any habit, breaking the pattern of over-apologizing requires practice.

Depending on your unique circumstances, you may wear more than one mask at any given time or wear one not listed here.

Knowing the characteristics of the various masks can help you identify when you are wearing one of them. Identifying these masks should not be seen as criticizing or blaming your family. Instead, once you are aware of the mask(s) you wear, take the opportunity to change it or take it off. As the renowned poet Maya Angelou has said, "When we know better, we do better."

Unmasking the Authentic You

"Always be a first rate version of yourself, instead of a second rate version of somebody else."

— Judy Garland

Authenticity is a technical term used in the philosophy of art and psychology. A common definition for being authentic is: attempting to live one's life according to the needs of one's inner being, rather than the demands of society or one's early conditioning.

Being authentic can also be described as perceiving one's self, others, and even things in a radically new way. Some writers argue that authenticity also requires self-knowledge and that it will alter (usually enhance) a person's relationships with other people.

You may have heard people being described as "the real deal" or "genuine." Similar to the computer acronym, WYSIWYG (*what you see is what you get*), authenticity is genuine, bona fide, natural, and confident. In all likelihood, the person described portrays a life of authenticity and integrity.

Your authenticity is what you unabashedly present to the world. It's not simply your name, job status, whom you marry, where you live, or what school you attended. It's not a label you wear like a designer tag sewn into your latest outfit. Authenticity is living your life with integrity every day and in every situation.

We live in a culture where names and labels are assigned to identify individuals and groups; unfortunately, these labels are often stereotypes assigned that do not tell us who these people really are. Stereotypes create expectations in people about who people are. For example, society has always assigned names or labels to women that are laden with expectations. We become defined as the: mother, wife, sister, friend, daughter, aunt, cousin, grandmother, and mother-in-law. The names we give and accept ultimately shape who we believe we are, and they come overloaded with limitations and preconceived expectations.

For example, wives "should" be in charge of the home interior; mothers "should" nurture; sisters "should" be loyal; daughters "should" be obedient;" aunts "should" be permissive; grandmothers "should" be cuddly, and on and on. These "shoulds" more often than not define who we ultimately become.

⚠️

CAUTION:
"Should" = unrealistic
expectations of yourself or others

I literally cringe when I hear brilliant, talented, successful women introduce themselves as "Tommy's mom," "Bob's wife," or "Margie's sister." When you introduce yourself that way, what does it tell the other person about who YOU are? You certainly may be some of those things, but you are much more than the labels society assigns you.

Is that really how you want to be identified?

Labels become challenging when we attach the concept of our identity to these roles and respond to the world and other people based on a false identity.

27

You are much more than a label!

When I was a younger woman, I was often guilty of accepting labels instead of expressing myself authentically. My shyness, lack of confidence, and fear of being noticed kept me stuck in roles that didn't accurately define me. I played roulette with my identity to fit in and be accepted. Stepping outside my self-imposed box and learning to define myself was an ongoing struggle. I was afraid to let anyone know how I truly felt or what I wanted.

Consequently, I was unable to be spontaneous and or participate in experiences that could have enhanced my life tremendously (e.g., walking up to someone and introducing myself or going back to school).

To the outside world, it looked like I had it all together. I dressed well, showed up when expected, and was a "good girl." Yet, deep inside, I felt like a fraud. Something was missing. I just didn't know what it was or where to look for it.

In my quest to find answers, I stumbled upon the book *The Dance of Anger* by Harriet Lerner, Ph.D. This book was my first peek into the roles women are conditioned to play in relationships and the anger buried beneath those expectations.

I learned that I could be genuine, uniquely genuine—I could speak up for what I wanted without fear of ridicule, censorship, or dismissal. I learned to ask for what I wanted honestly and assertively. I learned that being myself is not a bad thing. I learned that I am unique and I don't have to edit who I am. I realized I didn't have to live by the labels and expectations others felt were right for me. I learned how to be my authentic self. I learned to use the genie within to empower myself rather than hold me back.

Are you expressing your authentic self?

Let's look at some things that may keep you from being authentic:

Being indecisive: Indecisiveness is frequently connected to lack of self- confidence and a predisposition to worry about potential problems. Not making a decision or choice leaves the door open for others to make choices and decisions on your behalf. And, even when you don't make a decision, there will be consequences of your inaction. When asked to make a decision or choice, please don't ever say: "I don't know" or "It doesn't matter." Everything matters and you always have a choice. When you respond in this way, you're saying to the world: "I lack confidence," "I'm out of touch with my feelings," or "I'm fearful you won't like or accept what I think." Meanwhile, the real you, your authentic self, slips further into the abyss.

People will value you only as much as you value yourself.

Lowering expectations of self and others: People will value you only as much as you value yourself. Any woman who has ever been introduced as "Tommy's mom" or "Bob's wife" has experienced the feeling of disconnect between her true self and the introduction. And whether that feeling is verbalized or not, accepting how others define you gives them permission to categorize you and diminish your authentic self.

Believing that other people's wishes come first: Historically, women have been raised to take care of others before taking care of themselves. It saddens me to hear women say, "My children come first." Of course, we love our children and want what is best for them. But if you're not taking care of yourself, how will you have the stamina to take care of your children?

There is a reason the flight attendant tells you to put on your oxygen mask first in case of an emergency; it's so you will be able to aid your seatmate—it's not because you're being selfish! In fact, the word *selfish* has become a dirty word. Taking care of yourself first is not selfish—it's a selfless act that will empower you. Creating time in your busy schedule for self-care is crucial if you are to continue giving of your time, energy, and resources. Schedule some "me time" on your calendar at least once a week.

Hesitating about new experiences: Be open to trying new experiences. If you always take the same route home, take a different road. You may find a babbling brook or a field of wildflowers. Try new things, such as a sport, a hobby, or a different kind of cultural event. You might discover your passion this way, even a new career.

Using negative language about yourself: Be careful of the words you use to describe yourself. Calling yourself derogatory names (i.e., stupid, dumb, fat, loser, etc.) sends an internal message, which forms a negative belief. Instead, use power words and phrases to express yourself. For example, when someone asks you to take on a task or perform a chore, you can say, "I have other plans" instead of "Oh, I'm sorry, I can't." When you say, "I can't," you leave yourself open to "why?" questions and you may feel the need to offer an explanation when it's not necessary.

Dishonoring commitments to yourself: Today, make a commitment to yourself that you know will make a difference in your life. For example, commit to writing in your journal at least once a week, commit to exercising three times a week, or commit to scheduling a manicure at least once a month. Whatever you decide, honor the commitment you make to yourself!

One Word That Hinders Authenticity

If you find your conversations peppered with *should*, as in "I *should* make the beds" or "I *should* exercise," it means you are trying to appease someone or you are doing something you really don't want to do. (After all, if you truly wanted to exercise, you would.)

In other words, you are being dishonest about what you really want. You are not being real or truthful with yourself or anyone else.

Three Questions Guaranteed to Keep You on the Path to Authenticity

Anytime you doubt whether you're being authentic when someone requests your time, energy, or resources, ask yourself these three questions:

1. *Is it good for me?* We all use creative ways to get our needs met. But if you ask me to do something that is good for you, it might not be good for me. It might be something that will require more time, energy, or sacrifice than I want to give. If I say, "No," I don't need to feel guilty about making a choice based on what's best for me.

2. *Is it good for the person making the request?* For example, someone might ask you to take part in a cover up for an error he made. Of course, it very well might be helpful to him in the short-term, but you would be putting your reputation and integrity on the line. Jump back to question #1: Is it good for me? It's great to help other people, but if it's going to stop you from doing what you

32

want or enjoy, costs you time and energy you don't have, or infringes on your personal integrity, it may not be worth it. Of course, weigh the long-term benefits and the relationship you have with that person. You may not want to help your children with their homework, but you know your life and their lives will be better long-term if they do well in school.

3. ***Do I want to do it?*** How many times do you take on a project, commitment, or chore you really don't want to do just to appease someone else? There's nothing wrong with saying, "Gee, I won't be able to accommodate that request" or "That's just not something I am willing to take on."

If your answer to any two of these questions is "NO," then don't do it. If you do it anyway, and you end up harboring anger, resentment, frustration, or doubt over doing it, then you're slowly eroding your authenticity.

Your Unique Divine Natural Attributes

Each person is endowed with his or her own scientifically identifiable, unique DNA. Scientific DNA, or deoxyribonucleic acid, is found in the nucleus of a cell. DNA testing can provide links to ancestry, prove paternity, reunite adoptees with birth parents, and provide forensic evidence in criminal cases.

Scientifically, DNA is the genetic code for all life forms.

However, I'd prefer to think of DNA another way.

I define DNA as your unique *"Divine Natural Attributes."* Your unique Divine Natural Attributes hold the answers to all your questions and the key to your success. For some people, this "DNA" may come from a Higher Power, the Universe, or God. Whatever belief system you have, it likely involves some degree of belief that a greater force influences your life. And that belief hinges on the fact that you already have everything you need—you are hard-wired to live with purpose, joy, and abundance.

The possibilities entering your mind would never occur if you didn't already have what you need to fulfill your highest potential.

Your unique "DNA" is programmed for success, prosperity, and abundance. So why not tap into that energy and align yourself with what the universe has waiting for you?

Just like the developer who provides the code to run your computer, the universe has programmed your codes. And, similar to the computer, you can easily access the codes once you are familiar with the process.

For example, when you are not in harmony with the words you speak, the actions you take, and the beliefs you hold, you leave yourself open to frustration, indecisiveness, anger, and doubting your self-worth. But once you know how to embrace your unique DNA, you have the roadmap to living a joyful, authentic life.

I know from personal experience that the universe divinely orchestrates a life plan for us. And no matter how we may let life get in the way and stray us from that plan, it's never too late to get back into harmony with it. For example, from an early age I had a penchant for helping people sort out, explore, and redefine what they wanted most. And while I let life get in the way of achieving my dream of becoming a psychologist, I always knew I would end up in a helping profession. The inner urging, the relentless promptings, and the desire were always there. I knew that one day I would achieve my dream. And I did. That reinforces my belief that the universe had already divinely orchestrated my life plan.

Your unique "DNA" is programmed for success, prosperity, and abundance!

You are no different; your unique Divine Natural Attributes are waiting for you to tap into them so you can live your absolute best life.

Now, use the table below to hone in on your unique Divine Natural Attributes. Review your innate talents, the things you enjoy, and what you are passionate about to formulate a picture of your unique DNA. List everything you can think of without editing or censoring. Think about what limiting thoughts (such as not good enough, too old/young, not smart enough) keep you from trusting your choices, and put those thoughts aside. Look at the things that keep coming up for you in your life, the thoughts you have about what is possible, and begin to access your unique DNA. List them all—no matter how lofty they may seem. If you need more space, use a piece of paper—I hope your list is long.

Things I've Always Wanted To Do	My Talents/ Gifts	Things I Enjoy Doing Now

Now take a long, honest look at your list. Is it in alignment with what you are doing now? If not, perhaps you can revisit a time when what you were doing brought insurmountable joy and you felt fulfilled and at peace.

In what other ways could you use your gifts?

Maybe your talent is teaching. Can you teach others to do what you enjoy?

Perhaps you are a good listener. Could you use your listening skills to become a counselor, mentor, or coach?

You can tap into your Unique DNA to transform the things you enjoy doing into what you now know to be your life purpose.

You're now familiar with some of the masks we use to hide our true selves. List here, the masks you will shed and what you will do to uncover your true self?

_____

_____

_____

_____

_____

_____

CHAPTER 2

Set Strong Boundaries to Balance Your Life

"Your boundary is the invisible fence you put up to insulate yourself from taking on more, doing more, and trying to be more. Your boundaries help create balance in your life."

— *Gladys M. Anderson*

Creating balance in your life is a process of making choices, setting clear, consistent boundaries, and deciding what works best for you. Creating balance should not add to your stress level.

Look at balance this way:

Imagine you are a juggler keeping five balls in the air. Name them: work, family, health, friends, and spirit. You're keeping all of these in the air.

One ball—work—is made of rubber. You soon discover that if you drop it, it will bounce back.

The other four balls are made of glass; these are family, health, friends, and spirit. Remember, if you drop the rubber ball, it will bounce back. But if you drop one of the glass balls—family, health, friends, or spirit—it will be irreversibly marked, nicked, damaged, or even shattered. It will never be the same.

What you must understand when you are striving for balance is: You may find it easy to juggle all the balls, but the ball you let fall creates imbalance in your life.

How to Keep All the Balls in the Air Without Losing Sight of What's Important

Here's a reality check. With all the balls you're juggling every day, is it realistic to expect that you won't drop one (or two) every now and then? That demanding trek up the mountain of responsibilities has become your way of life.

Don't beat yourself up when you drop a ball. Just rearrange the balance.

Take a look at this example. Your hours may be different, so use whatever is realistic for you.

Sleep	8 hrs.
Work and Commuting	10 hrs.
Chores	2 hrs
Exercising	1 hr
Family Time	2 hrs.
Social Networking/Computer Time	2 hrs.
Friends	1 hr.
TOTAL	26 hrs.

That's 26 hours, and you know there are only 24 HOURS IN A DAY.

With a schedule like that, no wonder you feel overwhelmed. There's no time for self-care.

Let's take a closer look at each of the "balls" individually to see how you can adjust your balance so you can keep your balls in the air, at least most of the time.

Work

On average, we work nearly nine full weeks (350 hours) LONGER per year than our peers in Western Europe do.

Most Americans are putting in longer hours on the job now than we did in the 1950s.

Maintaining boundaries between home and work is an ongoing struggle for many women. That is especially true in today's electronic age where instant access to people and information (through smartphones, instant messages, email, Twitter, Facebook, and countless other gadgets) is right at your fingertips—literally. Maintaining boundaries for busy women is one of those "nice if you can get it" things, but it doesn't always seem practical or even realistic in today's busy world. However, no matter how much you love your work, you still need a break from all the connections.

Family and Friends

Does your family's schedule feel like a road race? Are you constantly juggling schedules, activities, and appointments?

Our children are being shuffled daily from one activity to another. We're trying to fit in doctor appointments, hairdresser/barber appointments, trips to the supermarket, going to the gym, and keeping track of everybody in the family. No wonder we struggle to balance it all.

I watch helplessly as my daughter, a single parent to a fourteen-year old son, juggles work, home, parenting, and other activities while putting her self-care on the back burner.

But the more she gives, the less time she has to recharge, to find balance. And this imbalance affects how she handles work, the home, and her family. My daughter is not the only woman caught in this cycle where everything and everyone takes priority over taking care of herself.

While it is certainly important to spend time with family and friends, it's equally important to spend time rejuvenating and refocusing on YOU! Put at least one self-care task on your endless "To-Do" list.

Health

Without good heath, all the other balls are meaningless. If you don't have good health, you won't have the energy to be successful at work, take care of your family, or connect with your spirit. Get enough sleep, exercise regularly, or spend time meditating.

Did you know that people who get seven to nine hours of sleep per night generally have higher productivity, feel more energetic throughout the day, and experience less stress?

Sleep is crucial for concentration, memory formation, and repairing and rejuvenating the body's cells. Both mentally and physically, a good night's sleep is essential for your health and your energy.

Seven to nine hours per night may seem unrealistic with today's busy lifestyles, but even a small change such as going to bed a half hour earlier can have a positive effect on your body and your health. Set a goal of going to bed thirty minutes earlier than usual.

Exercise is also important for good health. You may not always have the time or financial resources for an expensive gym membership. But you can walk around your neighborhood or take advantage of one of the many at-home exercise programs on CD.

Exercising for thirty to sixty minutes in the comfort of my home fits into my busy schedule without the expense and time involved of going to the gym. Of course, if you like going to the gym and that's what works for you, by all means, join one. The important thing is that you do something to keep fit.

Nurturing Spirit

If you are too busy—consumed every day by your projects, your uncertainty, your craving—how can you find the time to stop and look deeply into the situations in your family, community, and nation?

I've heard many people say, "I'm too busy to think." What that implies is that they are so overwhelmed with juggling all the day-to-day balls that they have no energy left to think deeply about anything outside of what's immediately in front of them.

Practice taking some quiet time to meditate, pray, or think deeply to gain focus and clarity.

Unwind From Your Busy Day

I know there are reports to write, dinners to cook, laundry to wash, children to chauffeur—PTA, shopping, cleaning, and an endless array of activities filling your days. Although busy lives can be interesting and rewarding, being overly busy can wear you down, stress you out, and even make you sick. The way to beat your addiction to being busy is to understand your own limits, set priorities, learn to say, "No," and stop to smell the roses.

Most women tend to feel guilty about taking time to unwind or engage in self-care. When you make self-care a priority, you nourish your body, soul, and spirit and can return to your obligations energized, refreshed, and ready to give to your family, community, and the world.

Perhaps guilt could not get a foothold if you realized taking time for yourself gives you more energy to devote to the ones you love.

When I worked full-time, I often walked into the house, started making dinner, asked my daughter whether she had done her homework, and listened to my husband unload his stressful day all at once.

I finally realized that I left myself no time to unload *my* stressful day. I was on the go from the minute I walked into the house. I decided I needed some down time. So, I informed my family that I needed to take the first fifteen to twenty minutes after I got home to "unwind." I still take fifteen to twenty minutes to unwind at the end of each workday, even though there's just my husband and me at home now. If you work full- or part-time, or work from home, this fifteen to twenty minute "break" is a wonderful way to release the stress of your workday and recharge your batteries.

In addition to your daily "break," build leisure time into your weekly schedule. Make time to relax and rejuvenate with friends—have fun without feeling guilty.

Give Up the Superwoman Role

Give up trying to be the perfect partner, the perfect employee, the perfect hostess, the perfect parent, the perfect daughter, or the perfect friend. It is not possible.

But so what if you never throw a party like Martha Stewart, the home decorating guru, organize your workspace like a professional organizer, or empty your inbox?

What you can do is accept the situation as it is. There is such a thing as "good enough," and when you've done your best, it's good enough. Relinquish the notion that you can do all, and be all things to everyone in your life.

You are NOT Superwoman. Remember, Superwoman has superhuman strength and can fly—and she is not real.

Real women need to set boundaries on their time, their "chores," their lives. If you let others control your time and resources, you open the floodgates to stress, anxiety, and frustration. Instead of being nice and accommodating, you're really teaching other people that they have the power to determine how, when, and what you spend your time doing. The role of Superwoman is a clever way of wearing the mask of perfection.

Revise the Expectations You Place on Yourself

Maybe you grew up believing that it's better to give than to receive, and consequently, you give and give, yet you have difficulty receiving (e.g., compliments, gifts).

Look at where these expectations come from. Are they cultural, family defined, or self-imposed? Don't let someone else's expectations become your reality.

Set your own expectations about what you are willing to do and give.

So What If You Make the Wrong Turn?

You don't have to know every detail before taking action.

When you spend precious time trying to figure out every possible outcome to the decisions you make, you are actually agonizing over things you have no control over. Sometimes you just have to make a decision and go with it. If it turns out you could have made a better choice, revise or change your approach.

We all have the power of choice, whether we're deciding what to have for dinner, whether we should get married or have children, or how we react to life's circumstances.

We've all taken the "wrong" turn and often regretted our decision.

But beating yourself up and grumbling about "what could have been" serves no purpose other than to keep you mired in dissatisfaction and engulfed in anxiety, depression, and guilt.

If you allow yourself to base your choices solely on your comfort level, you risk not taking the necessary steps to self-discipline and rob yourself of the chance to grow and move forward.

When you stretch yourself, you get out of your comfort zone and into what may at first feel a little uncomfortable, but you begin to build self-confidence. You can easily gauge your growth by the amount of discomfort you feel.

The more we do things we aren't comfortable doing, the more we are able to do.

Every choice we make influences our next choice. When we make one choice that we regret and continue to dwell on it, our next choice is affected. And on and on the cycle goes until we become afraid to make any decision, which leads to even more self-doubt and fear.

Trust your instincts. Everything does not have to be in a logical sequence. Some decisions are based more on instinct, such as whether you should get the green car or the red one. Which one feels right to YOU?

There is no wrong choice—only different choices.

But don't be tempted to go with self-indulgent desires because it "feels right," only afterwards to attempt to justify and rationalize your choice.

Weigh the pros and cons of your decision. Visualize living with your decision. Remember, some of your choices may not make sense to other people and that's okay. Most groundbreaking decisions in the fields of science and medicine were first met with skepticism and uncertainty.

There is no wrong choice—only different choices. So, don't beat yourself up if you make a "wrong" decision. Consider it a learning experience and gain knowledge from it. After all, you are human!

Your self-care is a critical step in the process to reveal your true self. What self-care practices will you commit to implementing to renew your mind, body and spirit? List them here:

_____

_____

_____

_____

_____

_____

CHAPTER 3

Invisible Woman No More

"I was slightly brain damaged at birth, and I want people like me to see that they shouldn't let a disability get in the way. I want to raise awareness—I want to turn my disability into ability."

— Susan Boyle

What does it mean to be invisible? By definition it means hidden, blurred, unseen, concealed, or obscured from view—in other words, rendered inconspicuous.

Some studies suggest that many women who feel invisible crave praise and acknowledgment from others.

However, I don't think it's as much about wanting praise and validation as it is about self-worth. Your idea of self-worth is based on what you believe others think about you.

Your self-worth is inborn. Children do not come into the world believing they aren't good enough, smart enough, or talented enough. Many parents have watched proudly as their children took to the stage to perform in musicals, school plays, and dance recitals. Do you think any of these children thought they couldn't sing, dance, or play their musical instruments? No, of course not, because they observed their families and teachers cheering them on and supporting their efforts. They had not yet learned to doubt their observations and experiences.

It's not until you experience a negative comment or rejection that your once positive outlook and self-worth take on a new meaning. And, once you buy into other people's observations and meanings you allow them to develop into your belief about yourself. The meanings you attach to your self-worth are based on your observations and experiences. Other people might convey their observations to you, but the meanings you attach to those observations are yours.

Remember Susan Boyle who made headlines when she appeared as a contestant on the TV show *Britain's Got Talent* singing - the British equivalent to our *American Idol?* Susan surprised the judges and most of the world with her rendition of *"I Dreamed a Dream"* from the musical, Les Misérables.

As I watched the show, I couldn't help but notice the smirks on the faces of the judges and their disinterested body language as Susan took the stage.

And because the judges didn't see Susan as the model image of standardized beauty—tall, perfect size 10—it seemed to me that she was dismissed as a viable contestant even before she sang one note.

I choose to see Susan as a confident woman who knew her value and didn't allow others' observations to sway her belief in her talent.

We have no control over how others view us, but it's much more important how you view yourself. When you hide your knowledge, talents, gifts, and interests, you're shortchanging the world and setting yourself up to be invisible.

Do you think Susan would have gotten up on that stage if she were concerned about how her dress looked? Do you think she mulled over whether or not her hair was in place or her nails were perfectly manicured?

I don't think so.

Susan Boyle didn't allow other people's observations to hold her back. She knew she had an exceptional voice and wanted to share it with the world; she wasn't concerned about the observations the judges on *Britain's Got Talent* made about her. Their smirks and snide comments didn't matter.

Susan Boyle suddenly is no longer invisible because she has shown the world what an exceptional voice she has. The moment she went on stage, the inner Susan was made visible to the world.

Suddenly Susan isn't invisible anymore, but the world's fascination with outward appearances has not helped to conquer the problem of the invisible woman. We all need to step up like Susan Boyle did and own who we truly are.

But what if you're thinking, "I'm just an ordinary woman without any exceptional talent"?

Squash that thought right now.

None of us are invisible; nor should we let anyone treat us as invisible women.

Your talents and gifts may be buried beneath the fears and doubts you have, but they are there if you are willing to become visible. You are a gifted, knowledgeable, interesting, loving, compassionate woman. If you need help uncovering all you have to offer to the world, you might benefit from a few coaching sessions to get you on your way.

Loving the Woman in the Mirror

Each morning at some point as you start your day, I'm sure you look in the mirror. The woman who looks back at you must be able to accept herself as she is—warts and all.

When you look in the mirror it's the perfect time to start building a reserve of confidence and self-worth by dispelling some of the invisibility beliefs you have.

You know that saying, "Beauty is in the eye of the beholder." Just imagine if you really believed that to be true and the woman in the mirror confirmed it? How would your day go? Would your spirits be lifted as you go about your day?

You can become your own personal cheerleader each day as you look in the mirror.

None of us are invisible; nor should we let anyone treat us as invisible women.

A cheerleader is a lot like your magical genie who grants your every wish. Ask your genie to encourage you, applaud your successes, and pump you up when you're ready to throw in the towel.

You can also begin loving the woman in the mirror when you "*act as if*…." By that, I mean you can practice scenarios and look for situations where you can show off your confidence, talents, and visibility—e.g., look in the mirror and act "as if" you are confidently giving a speech or act as if you are effortlessly working the crowd at a networking meeting. This type of self-talk will quickly build confidence, and before long, you will be comfortable enough to tackle the most challenging undertaking.

Whenever I had a class or occasion where I had to speak in front of a group, it's a wonder no one heard my knees knocking—that's how afraid I was. But by practicing in front of a mirror, I became confident and secure that I could deliver flawlessly.

Another way to love the woman in the mirror is by becoming the shepherd and not the sheep. A shepherd leads her flock and knows where she wants to go. Be a rebel, set your own trends, make and be comfortable with your own fashion statement.

At one time, (before I learned to love the woman in the mirror), I looked in my closet and noticed almost everything I owned was beige or some variant of beige.

Beige is boring! I discovered that, for me, I was subconsciously hiding behind a non-descript color to camouflage my true self. To me, the color beige screams, "Don't notice me!" I was playing it safe, or so I thought. There's nothing wrong with beige if you like it, but if you are using it to hide your true self, then it becomes just another mask you wear to be invisible.

Today, my wardrobe looks much different. I choose vibrant, bold colors as often as I like. And if I do decide to wear beige, I complement it with bright colors. Colors make me feel alive and daring.

If you aren't loving the woman you see in the mirror, I encourage you to invest in yourself and stop waiting in the wings. You are an extraordinarily beautiful, well-hidden treasure just waiting to be revealed.

CHAPTER 4

An Attitude of Gratitude Attracts More Abundance

"Gratitude unlocks the fullness of life. It turns what we have into enough, and more. It turns denial into acceptance, chaos to order, and confusion to clarity. It can turn a meal into a feast, a house into a home, a stranger into a friend. Gratitude makes sense of our past, brings peace for today, and creates a vision for tomorrow."

— Melody Beattie

Is your glass half-empty or half-full? Your answer may reflect whether or not you have an optimistic or pessimistic attitude.

People who view the glass as half-full tend to think more positively and look on the brighter side. Pessimists are inclined to see the worst-case scenario and focus more on what is wrong or could go wrong.

Our media outlets bring us the most devastating news, throwing in one or two positive stories for "balance." We are so primed to pay attention to all the terrible events happening around us and in our lives that we often ignore the things that are going well for us.

For example, you finished your project on time, but you overlooked one minor detail. The error does not change that you've done a good job. If you beat yourself up about one little detail, you are discounting the great work you did.

Events are not stressful. Our perceptions and attitudes provide the stress. In the popular book, *The Secret*, numerous well-known contributors shared a recurrent theme: "We are what we think." Our thoughts are powerful tools. We should use them to our advantage.

Develop an attitude of gratitude!

I'm sure you remember your parents saying, "Count your blessings," and other phrases urging you to be grateful. Your parents weren't just spouting idle words; they were trying to get you to develop an attitude of gratitude.

Every once in a while, it is good to take stock of just how good we have it. Take a look at some of the things we are blessed with:

Free Time

Most of us complain about being busy and not having enough time, yet the typical American has more time than ever before. According to the U.S. Census Bureau you have more than five hours a day of free time. That's an increase of nearly an hour since 1965 and a gain of nearly four hours since the nineteenth century. While experts say that by 2050, the average workweek will be just twenty-seven hours, I wonder how the increased use of technology will affect these numbers. I recall when the first computer was introduced in the company where I worked. We were told it would greatly reduce our workload. And, while the computer was faster, I soon discovered the work demands were greater—e.g., easy access to requests via email, more forms to fill out and more reports to be compiled. Even with these expert predictions, I know you're not waiting until 2050 for more free time! I will suggest, however, that you take a serious look at what you are doing with your time.

I'm sure if you give it some thought, you can carve out at least one of those extra four hours to take some time to relax, refocus, and rejuvenate yourself. Be grateful that you have as much time as you do, and show that gratitude by using it wisely and to the best advantage.

Our Gadgets

Do you have a Smartphone, computer, access to the Internet, TV, or a microwave? Most of us take our gadgets for granted instead of showing gratitude for the technology that powers these nifty tools.

Recently when our town experienced a power outage for several days, I became acutely aware of how much I took my cellphone, computer, and electricity for granted. That's at least three more things I can add to my gratitude list daily. I hope you don't have to experience a power outage to show gratitude for your electricity and for the tools that help keep your life running smoothly.

Reading

I am and always have been an avid reader. Friends often want to engage me in what's going on in the latest episode of *American Idol* or some other TV show, and they are shocked when I say I don't watch it. I find reading much more enjoyable than television. It's a privilege to be able to read.

Did you know that in 1970 barely half the people in the world were literate and many of them could afford only a few books?

Today, more than 80 percent of the world's people can read. Reading is a wonderful way to travel, learn, and grow. With the emergence of the Internet, no book, reference material, or information is out of your reach. The vast network of booksellers means that there is always someone, somewhere who will provide the books you are looking for. And, of course, there is always your local library to browse.

Consider joining or starting a book club with a group of friends for relaxation, good conversation, and connection.

Since you're reading this, count yourself blessed to read these pages. The gift of reading is a staple on my gratitude list.

A Room of Your Own

Even with so many people facing foreclosure and struggling to keep their homes, many of us still have plenty to be thankful for when we walk through our front door. In 1950, the typical home had only one floor with usually no more than 1,000 square feet, one bathroom, and cost $14,500.00. Today we live in two and three story homes, have at least one and a half baths, and can afford to (and do) pay much more than $14,500 for them! Count your blessings!

Memories

We have digital photos and videos to remind us of our best personal memories and the Internet to help us remember which year the blizzard hit and who sang a particular popular song.

We don't need a scribe to record our histories.

Today, with all the modern media tools, we can have access to a record of our lives to pass to our descendants, to comfort us as we age, and to remind us of the important milestones in our lives. A nifty tool for recording your ancestors, descendants, events, and even pictures is Family Tree Maker, a genealogy software program created by Ancestry.com. Be grateful for you precious memories and start sharing them with your loved ones now.

Music

Music is said to "calm the savage beast." Relaxing, calming music also has been shown to lower blood pressure and decrease anxiety. Another way to benefit from music is to share a happy tune.

By that, I mean get into the habit of sharing at least one happy message each day with someone. Instead of complaining and lamenting a sad song about what is wrong, you can acknowledge gratitude for the song in your heart, and by doing so, you may just lift someone else's spirit.

We all get bombarded with dark clouds—doom and gloom news reports, unemployment statistics, crime, and economic disasters. Yet, even with all of that, there is plenty to be grateful for. So, go ahead, show gratitude for that happy tune in your heart and you may just dance away on a happier note!

"When you are grateful, fear disappears and abundance appears."

— Anthony Robbins

In his book, *Thanks*, Dr. Robert A. Emmons describes research he carried out that shows that people who express their gratitude daily are 25 percent happier and healthier than those who don't—and it only takes a few minutes a day!

Showing gratitude could help you sleep better, feel less depressed and more energetic, exercise more, live a more satisfying life, and help you live longer. All of that from just being grateful, according to Drs. Blair and Rita Justice of the *Health Leader*, the online Wellness Newsletter.

If you don't already have a gratitude journal, I encourage you to start one now. It only takes a few minutes a day to jot down at least five things for which you are grateful.

Here are some gratitude tips to get you started:

- I am grateful for enough food to sustain me.

- I am grateful for the rain because it nourishes the soil.

- I am grateful for time to connect with my loved ones.

- I am grateful that I can write and read.

- I am grateful for fresh air to breathe.

Throughout the day, look for things to be grateful for—a beautiful flower in bloom, the smell of freshly cut grass, the smile on the face of a loved one, the unexpected phone call or compliment.

When you develop the habit of being grateful for what you already have, the door of abundance opens wide. No matter how bad things may appear, there's always a silver lining. It's much easier to see the silver lining when you adopt an attitude of gratitude. Close the door on negative thinking and open the door to abundance.

Everything you need and want will be made available when you need it, in the way you need it.

And the best part is that you don't have to figure out HOW it will manifest itself. Your job is simply to believe!

"Every person naturally wants to become all that they are capable of becoming; this desire to realize innate possibilities is inherent in human nature; we cannot help wanting to be all that we can be."

— Wallace Wattle

Let me give you a personal example of how gratitude leads to abundance in life, even in the times when it might seem most difficult to be grateful.

When the office where I worked for seventeen years suddenly closed its doors, I felt as though I had been thrown out to sea without a lifeline.

You see, I had never figured out what I wanted to be when I grew up. As a result, I had spent many years supporting someone else's dream, while mine simmered on the back burner. I didn't even really believe I had a dream. My dreams were buried underneath all the doubts, fears, what if's, and limiting beliefs I was holding onto.

But when that job ended and that door closed, I came to realize the universe had just presented me with the opportunity to return to school for the degree in counseling psychology I had always secretly wanted. I instinctively knew it was now or never. I didn't waste any more time in the shallow end of the pool. I jumped into the deep end of the pool, confident I could swim the distance.

The universe, like a magical genie, is just waiting to grant your wishes

And once I wrapped my mind around the concept that it wasn't too late to live my dream, I embraced that thought with every fiber of my being and left everything else to the universe.

I didn't know how I was going to do it or exactly when it would happen—I just believed that it would. I didn't allow myself to focus on the details.

You may think this is unrealistic, but when you truly believe and focus more on the outcome than the details, the how will take care of itself, and that's exactly what happened for me.

I moved from regional office assistant to getting a master's degree in counseling psychology to managing my own successful coaching and therapy practices.

To get to my classes, I drove ninety miles each way through rain, sleet, and snowstorms in my bright yellow Toyota, which had many, many miles on it. And, I didn't miss a class! While I witnessed accidents on the highway, cars skidding in snow, I trudged along, believing I would make it home safely.

You see everything I needed—safety, money, gas, energy, a car to drive—everything was supplied for me. Had I spent time trying to figure out HOW I would get to my classes, how I would get through grad school, or how I would manage my family, I probably would have sabotaged myself. I would have gotten in my own way by interfering with what the universe had planned for me. Instead of worrying about the how, I turned my attention to all I had to be grateful for.

There is nothing unique about my story. You, too, have a story and are presented with opportunities and choices every day. How you choose to live out your stories and your beliefs with your unique abilities is the key to achieving what you want most.

You only have to believe in the outcome; then the universe, like a magical genie, is just waiting to grant your wishes.

You have value and you were put on this earth to share your unique gifts.

What are you willing to do to manifest your dream?

What beliefs do you hold that keep you stuck?

Are you ready to give up trying to figure out the "how" and focus your attention more on the outcome? If you can't figure out how, start with feeling gratitude for all you have and soon the universe will open up its doors of abundance so more reasons to be grateful will present themselves and move you toward your goals.

List a few things that you're grateful for:

_____

_____

_____

_____

_____

_____

_____

"The next 30 days are going to pass whether you like it or not, so why not think about something you have always wanted to try and give it a shot for the next 30 days?"

- Matt Cutts

CHAPTER 5

Exchanging Harmful Thoughts for Helpful Habits

"You are today where your thoughts have brought you; you will be tomorrow where your thoughts take you."

— James Allen

Carrie, wearing a stylish outfit with matching accessories, looked confident and serene as she spoke. When I said, "You're in control of your thoughts," she glanced over her designer glasses and looked at me as if I had suddenly sprouted a second head.

Carrie had just recounted to me the latest drama-filled event in her life. And although it had happened several months earlier, she could not stop thinking about it. She continued to agonize, brood over, doubt her decisions, and "what-if" the situation to death.

All of this drama resulted in Carrie becoming sad, sleeping poorly, being unable to concentrate and generally feeling tired most of the time.

Like Carrie, you may be repeating harmful patterns, spending time thinking about situations you have little or no control over. You may respond by telling me that you have no control over your recurring thoughts, but you do!

The Law of Attraction is a universal law much like the law of gravity. Simply stated, the law of gravity acts between everything in the Universe. The Law of Attraction says, *"You are what you think and you attract that which you focus on, or like attracts like."* If you haven't heard of the Law of Attraction (LOA) before, let me give you an example of how it works. According to the LOA, everything begins with a thought—whether the thought is negative or positive. There is no relationship, industry, or structure that didn't begin with a single thought. For example, if you're constantly worrying about having enough money, your thoughts are focused on not having enough money. As a result, you will attract situations where you're struggling with your finances. But if your thoughts are: "I have more money" or "I have enough money to meet my financial obligations," you will attract more money into your life.

You are what you think, and you attract that which you focus on

When you focus on lack and scarcity, you just attract more of the same because that's what you're focusing on. When you ruminate over "what could/

70

should have been," "what if," and "if only," you just attract more of the same, and that leads to more worry and stress.

You can find out more about the Law of Attraction in books like *The Secret* by Rhonda Byrne and *Ask and It is Given* by Jerry and Esther Hicks.

Worry focuses on what has already happened (the past) or what you think will happen (the future). You have no control over either one…so why worry about what has already happened or what may happen? This is a harmful pattern that erodes self-confidence and keeps you stuck in situations that create "drama" and confusion in your life.

"When you worry you make it double" is a line from Bobby McFerrin's a capella hit song, "Don't Worry, Be Happy." I think one of the reasons this song was such a hit was because so many people worry, but they found solace in the idea that they could be happy.

As popular as the song was, it wasn't created to address the harmful patterns that produce worry, and it didn't teach people how to manage anxiety or *how* to be happy.

You can't control the weather or natural disasters; neither can you control what others do or think. When your mind is filled with worry about things out of your control, you are knee deep in someone else's business. The only thing you can control is how you think about these occurrences.

In Katie Byron's book, *Loving What Is,* she states, "A thought is harmless unless we believe it. It's not our thoughts but our attachment to our thoughts that causes suffering." When we plant harmful thoughts, it's not long before we begin to see these thoughts form deep roots that eventually take over the landscape of our minds.

Harmful Thought-Patterns: Their Origins and How to Change Them

The seeds of harmful thought-patterns may have been sown very early in your development. Your thought-patterns and behaviors started with a thought that turned into a belief about yourself.

Perhaps you believe you are being assertive and don't recognize when you're monopolizing conversations or being bossy.

This thought-pattern can be harmful because your self-worth is connected to being seen, heard, and validated. However, you are really shooting yourself in the foot. Other people may think your behavior is egotistical, self-absorbed, or just plain rude. They won't recognize that you are trying to get your emotional needs met. Instead of loudly tooting your own horn, do as writers are advised to do—show, don't tell. Let your positive actions speak louder than the words you actually speak.

You may feel less than confident in social situations and fear you will be rejected, not accepted, or treated as not good enough. This thought-pattern is one of inadequacy. In this case, inadequacy simply refers to that deep down feeling of deficiency or lack and is usually accompanied by a fear of failure and low self-confidence.

For example, if you think you are "not good enough," you may find yourself holding back, not following your dream of becoming a great musician, self-sabotaging your efforts to succeed in business, or stuck in unfulfilling roles, relationships, or situations that don't honor who you are.

Helpful Habits that Improve Relationships

Often when problems arise, it's an indication of the underlying thoughts driving your behaviors.

Thoughts such as "my feelings aren't important," "I have to show how smart I am," and "I have to be strong" are just a communication dance where you are listening to the wrong music and stepping all over your own toes.

You can change this situation by creating helpful thoughts. In the following chart are examples of hurtful thoughts and how you can change them by rewording and rethinking them so they will be helpful.

Hurtful Thoughts	Helpful Thoughts
If I make a mistake, don't follow the rules, or change my mind, I'm a failure.	I have the right to change my mind as often as I like. I set my own expectations, rules, and vision for my life. I acknowledge my mistakes and learn from them.
I have to fix everyone's problems.	I am only responsible for my problems, and I can't fix anyone else or his or her problems.
I feel powerless, helpless, and trapped.	I have choices. I am capable, confident, and competent. I am free to experience new and exciting things.

Identifying the communication patterns you use to talk to yourself will allow you to catch and stop yourself when you have a hurtful thought so you can change it to a helpful one. As time goes by, you will find you have trained yourself to quit thinking the hurtful thoughts so only the helpful ones will surface into your mind. Then you will have the confidence to communicate effectively with yourself and others.

...Everything can be taken from a man but one thing; the last of the human freedoms—to choose one's attitude in any given set of circumstances, to choose one's own way.

— Victor Frankl

CHAPTER 6

Exposing Limiting Beliefs that Keep You Stuck in Fear

"What you believe is what you achieve. You become what you affirm: positively affirm your greatness, genius, and fullest potential."

— *Mark Victor Hanson*

Limiting beliefs are the messages we have learned and internalized from family, culture, groups, religion, and society. These are the scripts dictating how life *should* be. We incorporate these messages into our daily lives, and consequently, we do not live our best life.

We *are not* our self-limiting beliefs and our self-limiting beliefs *are not* who we are. Not at all. They are at most funhouse mirrors in which we glimpse a grotesque distortion of ourselves.

I know with my head that these false beliefs are not a true image of myself. These thoughts aren't true—I don't really believe them—because I've learned how false they are throughout my own (ongoing) journey.

When I've held one of these self-limiting beliefs, I've tried to prove it wrong and I've succeeded.

At the same time, I see constant evidence of how self-limiting beliefs hold people back. I see such evidence in the lives of the women I work with. These women are like hungry ragamuffins, whose noses are forever pressed against the window. They can see other people seated at life's banquet, but they believe they will never participate in the feast.

That is a false belief. They have no way of predicting the future. Their view of their world is simply darkened by a self-limiting belief that has all the trappings of reality.

The problem lies in the assumptions of the sufferer who holds the limiting belief. That person believes she has no real or unique value, gifts, or positive qualities. That's the nature of a limiting belief.

Women I have known who have endured an abusive relationship are often brainwashed into feeling they have little or no value. Understandably, they tend not to feel blessed at all.

Even when women who have experienced emotional abuse know, on a conscious level, they have abilities, worth, and value—even when friends, family, and colleagues reassure them of their self-worth—it has no bearing on their emotional world because they cannot come to using that self-worth to better their situations.

"Yes, but..." she will say, or she will think, "It doesn't make me feel better about myself," or "That's just not how I see myself."

Women who are weathering the storm of emotional abuse don't feel any pleasure in the good others see in them because they simply don't believe it. The only communications they truly receive are those that reinforce the negative beliefs they hold about themselves.

A limiting belief is merely a mask hiding your true self

It's an agonizing place to be stuck in such negative thought-patterns, and it's equally frustrating for the people who try to support them.

Working with other women's limiting beliefs recently took me back to my first personal coaching experience where I was the woman being coached....

At first when the core question, "What's holding you back?" came up, I couldn't even formulate an answer. I thought I was doing pretty well and nothing was holding me back.

But as I went deeper, I uncovered a limiting belief about not being good enough that kept me procrastinating, stuck, and unable to move forward. My limiting beliefs were holding me back!

A limiting belief is merely a mask hiding your true self. And when you allow a limiting belief to define your reality, you struggle futilely with a vision of the future that is crude, pessimistic, and false.

That vision will crush you daily. As long as you continue to regard yourself through the filter of self-limiting beliefs, you won't be able to see, feel, or hear your own personal genie when it shows up.

And yet, as soon as you turn your focus away from that distorted image, you see that you are a perceptive, creative, supportive, nurturing, dynamic, multi-talented, energetic woman. Those qualities, and many more, are who you truly are.

Anyone who has survived an abusive relationship and dug very deeply into her own mind has unearthed an enormous arsenal of personal resources and riches.

When you control limiting beliefs, you will be able to see your personal genie. And, once you see your genie, your treasures, blessings, and joys will continue to grow and the day will come when you are able to claim and rejoice in them.

Record any limiting beliefs you've uncovered on this page:

_____

_____

Chapter 7

The Most Important Relationship You Will Ever Have Is with YOURSELF

> *"The quality of your life is the quality of your relationships."*
>
> *— Anthony Robbins*

The most important relationship you'll ever have is the one you have with yourself. Relationships with partners, family, friends, and colleagues all hinge on the relationship you develop with yourself.

When your inner relationship suffers, all other connections fall short of being as effective as they could be.

For example, feeling undeserving can attract negative, unfulfilling relationships with people who constantly mistreat you.

Before I learned to value myself, to set strong boundaries, and to believe I deserved the best life has to offer, I often found myself in relationships that were energy draining, stressful, and full of drama.

One of my favorite songs is Nancy Wilson's "I've Never Been to Me." In the song, she sings about meeting kings and visiting exotic places, but she's never been free to be herself.

A lot of us are guilty of wanting the trappings of a successful life—the luxurious home, the fancy cars, the exotic vacations—but none of these frills will equate to happiness and personal freedom if you don't have an emotionally healthy relationship with yourself.

I'm not a mathematician, but I know enough about algebra to know that a common denominator is an attribute, characteristic, or element common to all members within a group.

YOU are the common denominator in all your relationships!

You are a vital element of any relationship you have and the role you play determines whether it's a healthy, thriving relationship or unhealthy and withering. Without relationships in your life, you would not know what upsets you, what excites you, when to make a choice that's in your best interest, or what things trigger an automatic negative or positive response in you. Understanding your needs and developing strong boundaries is an important part of relationship building.

The book *Getting the Love You Want: A Guide for Couples* by Harville Hendrix paints a very clear picture of how relationship dynamics play out in a marriage. Although Hendrix' book is a guide for couples, I believe those same dynamics are present in any relationship. For example, the same unmet emotional needs in a marriage are mirrored in friendships, in the workplace, and in every other social interaction.

As a marriage and family therapist and life coach, I fully understand how a problem in one relationship plays out in others, and I want you to become aware as well. Here's an example of a couple with unmet emotional needs:

June and Tim had been married for only eighteen months, but their relationship was already being adversely affected by unmet emotional needs. June grew up in a chaotic household where alcoholism was prevalent. Children who are exposed to an environment where alcoholism is common often resort to what is familiar; for example, June often heard her father and mother engage in shouting matches, each vying for control and nothing being resolved.

Tim described his family as kind, loving, and supportive. Upon further examination, however, Tim revealed that his family was simply polite; they rarely had disagreements, but they also rarely talked about their feelings.

Whenever June and Tim disagreed, June became loud and often resorted to name-calling in a futile attempt to be heard. Tim, on the other hand, was used to getting his needs met by being "Mr. Nice Guy"—avoiding conflict at all costs, stifling how he really felt, and suppressing his true thoughts. Without intervention, Tim and June's relationship was at risk.

I'm worthy and I matter

Over a period of several months as I worked with June and Tim, they not only gained an awareness of the driving force behind their unmet emotional needs, but they also learned to communicate their feelings honestly and clearly, ask for what they wanted, and set realistic expectations for each other. They saw a distinct shift in their relationship dynamics.

Here is another example of how unmet emotional needs can lead to self-sabotage:

Sara is an intelligent, hard-working woman who landed her dream job as a manager in an advertising agency. Although Sara is very good at what she does, her co-workers complain that she is a "control freak," doesn't allow them to do their jobs, has a "know it all attitude," and undermines their ability to make decisions that are clearly within their areas of responsibility.

Sara grew up in a family where she didn't feel she mattered; she resorted to controlling (what we would call bullying today) her younger sister to make herself feel recognized and important. Because Sara didn't receive validation and acceptance from her parents, she soon discovered that when she told her sister what to do and when and how to do it, she felt smart, respected, and capable. Sara went into adulthood unconsciously believing that she could get her needs met by bullying, controlling, and threatening others.

I'm sure you've seen this behavior.

Elements of the scenarios above are evident in any relationship where emotional needs are not met. This behavior is what is referred to as "childlike" because it is synonymous with "I want what I want and I want it NOW." The person's attempts to get her emotional needs met are then acted out in power struggles, complaints, or by creating chaos. Sara learned that she could be assertive without being hostile and micro-managing. With the use of some positive affirmations, a strong desire to change, and a profound shift in the way she viewed herself, Sara increased her self-confidence and began to recognize, validate, and affirm her own strengths and talents. And, ultimately, she was able to relinquish her attempts to get her needs met by controlling others.

Whatever forms your unmet needs take, rest assured the behaviors will eventually show up in any relationship you have—including the one you have with yourself.

Unmet emotional needs always leak out in negative behaviors.

Emotions are not good or bad. All emotions derive from one's circumstances, mood, or relationships with others. For our purposes here, let's look at two types of emotions: suppressed and repressed emotions.

Repressed emotions are the subconscious rejection of past painful feelings, memories, or thoughts. Sometimes, a person will bury these repressed emotions for many years in an attempt to "protect" him- or herself from experiencing pain. Often, women in emotionally abusive relationships repress their feelings in a futile attempt to avoid more abuse.

Suppressed emotions are those feelings that you are aware of and consciously make a choice not to think about or dwell on. For example, you are aware of being angry but choose not to address your anger.

Whether emotions are repressed or suppressed, we all need to experience healthy emotions on a regular basis so we will feel:

acknowledged	needed
appreciated	noticed
competent	understood
confident	valued
loved	worthy

Feeling deprived of any of the above feelings is an "unmet emotional need."

Counterproductive Behaviors that Provide a Temporary Fix For Unmet Emotional Needs

- Attempts to control or manipulate

- An attitude of superiority

- A quest for status, money, recognition

- Competiveness—trying to be the first, the smartest, the best, etc.

- Entitlement

- Reckless behaviors—drinking, using drugs

- People pleasing

All of these are attempts to show "I'm worthy" and "I matter." Yet, none of these fill the void. When we behave in ways that don't address our emotional needs, those behaviors often lead to relationship problems, health issues, and a host of other problems. Until you realize you have unmet emotional needs, you are powerless to change and you will never truly feel emotionally satisfied.

Before you read further, spend some time thinking about any emotional needs you have that may not be met.

In the space below, list them. (If you need more space or you are afraid of someone else picking up this book, find a safe place like a private notebook to write them in.) For each unmet emotional need, ask yourself how not getting that need met may have resulted in your engaging in controlling or other dysfunctional and unhelpful behaviors, and/or relationship problems you have had because of how you sought to get an emotional need met in an unhealthy way.

_____

_____

_____

_____

_____

_____

_____

_____

What can you do better in the future when you feel your emotional needs are not being met?

To get you started, here are some examples. Determine what the unmet emotional need is, and then apply the process to get the need met.

Unmet Emotional Need	How to Meet the Emotional Need
I feel I am not good enough.	Use positive affirmations such as "I am lovable and worthy" to combat negative thoughts that you are not enough.
I feel I "*have to*" do, be, and give.	Set your own strong, consistent boundaries around what you are willing and capable of doing and giving. Set realistic expectations for yourself.
I feel I need to show everyone how smart I am.	Validate your own strengths and talents. Once you are confident in your abilities, you lessen the need to receive validation from others.
I'm afraid to express my true thoughts and feelings....	Trust that what you think or say has value. Uncover where this unmet need comes from. Then create a new positive thought that bolsters your confidence.

"You, yourself, as much as anybody in the entire universe, deserve your love and affection."

— Buddha

Discarding Limiting Beliefs

Limiting beliefs are messages we have internalized from our family, culture, groups, religion, and society. These messages are thought-patterns imparted by well-meaning authority figures. They become the scripts we have in our heads about how we believe life "should" be for us and for others, standards by which we were reared, and from which we learned how to act, what to believe, and how to express or experience feelings.

However, when we internalize and follow these messages without question, the result often conflicts with our spirit. Let's take a closer look at some of the beliefs that limit us.

Examples of Limiting Beliefs:

I should never burden others with my problems or fears.

This belief is rooted in the message: You can't trust anyone to help you or be there for you. This message usually stems from your family of origin.

When you live your life around this kind of message, you usually don't trust people. You may refrain from asking for help when you need it, and you believe you have to be strong to survive.

I am intimately familiar with this belief! As a child, I often got the message that I couldn't count on the people who were supposed to love me. Consequently, I went into adulthood believing I couldn't count on anyone to help me and I had to take care of myself. This belief is dangerous because it leads to mistrust, and eventually, in my case, to the label of "strong"—she can handle it. Little did anyone know I longed for someone to step in and make it all better—to make me feel accepted and worthy.

I have to raise my voice in order to be heard and taken seriously.

Children who grow up in chaotic environments often resort to raising their voices as a way to prove that they matter and to be heard. Conflict becomes a way of life for them. This kind of belief can result in physical altercations, arrest, or even death.

I have to do everything perfectly.

This hidden message says you can't make a mistake or fail at anything because admitting you made a mistake is a sign of weakness or imperfection.

People who have internalized this message spend an inordinate amount of time trying to make the perfect decision, make the right choices, pick the "right" mate, and avoid showing any signs of making an error in judgment. Remember, making mistakes or not accomplishing something the first time is not failure; it's an opportunity to learn and grow. The only real failure is the failure to try.

I am not good enough.

This limiting belief hinges directly on your self-worth—how you see and think about yourself. Self-worth is the internal image you have of yourself—whether or not you believe you deserve to be happy, the level of trust you have in your decision-making, and the value you place on yourself, your abilities, and your wishes. A woman who has low self-worth tends to seek approval and answers outside of herself. She is usually her own worst critic because she fears she will be criticized, rejected, or seen as "less than...."

You are born with your self-worth intact. Your self-worth is based on the meaning you attach to your observations and experiences. Most likely, that meaning stems from the meaning you observed from the people around you.

Like most limiting beliefs, the belief of not being good enough is also formed early in our lives; it is a response to not getting our emotional needs met, and it has nothing to do with reality.

Here's something you can do now to start changing this limiting belief:

Begin a journal for seven days to keep track of the limiting thoughts you have about your self-worth

(e.g., "I don't know enough to…" "I'm too old/young/fat to…" "I'm not smart enough to…" "I can't decide…" etc.)

At the end of the seven days, put your journal aside for three days. This length of time is important because you want to revisit what you wrote with a fresh perspective.

When the three days are up, go back and look at what you have written. Now, you're ready to turn each belief into an encouraging, positive thought. For example, if you wrote "I don't know enough," reframe it into "I am willing to embrace my inborn knowledge and wisdom every day."

Turn your negative beliefs into encouraging, positive thoughts.

By starting with this one small change, you will have accessed the power to love, approve, and accept yourself from within.

I can't get angry.

This limiting belief teaches us that showing any kind of emotion is wrong and unacceptable.

People who have a strong belief that they can't show anger usually stifle other emotions as well and often are depressed and prone to ulcers and other illnesses.

93

For example, Molly was your typical "easygoing" kind of woman. She always appeared to be in a good mood, smiled a lot, and was usually pretty accommodating. Yet beneath that shell of cheerfulness was a very angry young woman. You see, Molly received the message early in her life that showing any kind of emotion was unacceptable in her family. She noticed that whenever her parents had a disagreement, they laughed it off, avoiding the situation and never bringing it up again. This behavior is **not** a good way to address anger.

As a result of Molly's upbringing, whenever Molly's boss or colleagues did something she didn't like, she would laugh it off and move on, all the while seething inside.

Unfortunately, such behavior often has the opposite result of its intent. Molly believes she is not allowed to get angry until she reaches "the last straw," and then she tends to explode with anger. Over time, Molly slowly learned to express her feelings, opinions, and needs by stating such things as "I'm not comfortable with…," "I feel…," "I don't agree with…," and discovered a much healthier way to release her anger.

I don't deserve to be happy, successful. I am not worthy.

This limiting belief is a big one because it severely limits your ability to take the necessary steps to be happy, successful, or productive.

When your beliefs are governed by fear, either consciously or unconsciously, you place restrictions on what you can have, do, or become.

Henry Ford once said, "If you think you can… or if you think you can't…you're right!" It all depends on what you believe about yourself.

Your thoughts are a direct path to your feelings. Your feelings affect your behavior. How you feel influences what you think, and when you keep thinking the same thing, confirming that thought as true, it becomes a belief, and when it becomes a limiting belief, it ends up limiting your thoughts and behavior.

Your beliefs determine what you think is or is not possible. More often than not, they prove to be self-fulfilling prophecies. Once a belief is formed, your mind works overtime to prove it right, even if the belief is something negative like "Nobody cares about me" or "I am a failure."

Most people are unaware of how limiting beliefs affect the choices they make and the careers they choose. And even fewer people realize they can change limiting beliefs into empowering thoughts.

For example, if you believe you shouldn't get angry even when you're upset, ask yourself, "How much distress and discomfort is this situation causing me?" If you are uncomfortable and distressed, the limiting belief that you can't show anger may have you stuck in fear of expressing your opinions and wishes.

In the space below, write down all the limiting beliefs you can think of—like "I can't have what I want," "I shouldn't get angry," "I can't trust anyone," "I'm not good enough," or "I don't deserve what I want." If you need more space, use a notebook.

_____

_____

_____

_____

_____

_____

_____

_____

_____

Now, look at how you usually respond in situations where your limiting beliefs show up. Ask yourself:

- Is this belief triggering guilt, fear of rejection, fear of failure or success, fear of showing weakness in my mind? Be brutally honest.

- Do I find it easier to avoid or ignore this belief rather than face it?

If any of these situations sound familiar, you are probably allowing an irrational belief to cloud your thinking.

Discover the Root of Your Limiting Beliefs

Before you can get rid of a limiting belief, it's helpful to understand why you hold that belief. For each limiting belief you have, ask yourself where that belief originated. Is the belief rooted in messages you've internalized from your family, church, society, or some other group?

Once you are aware of the source of limiting beliefs, you are in a better position to discard them. Just because a limiting belief was formed early in your life doesn't mean you can't change it.

What if the limiting belief is that you aren't "good enough"? You may find yourself always trying to prove you're worthy by joining groups or organizations where you have to prove you are worthy. Look at college hazing, for example, where as a condition for membership, students are required to perform acts that endanger their physical and emotional health or they are even bullied into performing illegal acts to prove their worth.

When you feel unworthy, your self-esteem is compromised. Low self-esteem causes you to draw irrational conclusions about what others do and say, such as "She doesn't like me," "She thinks I don't know what I'm talking about," or "She doesn't like what I'm wearing." Then you've just turned a limiting belief into your perception of reality.

Have you ever put on a new outfit and immediately felt confident and pretty? That's because your perception of your self-image changed.

You need to do the same thing with your self-limiting beliefs. Change them for beliefs that will help you achieve what you want in life by showing you are confident and comfortable with whom you are. Building a healthy, nurturing relationship with yourself is the most important relationship you'll ever have. Review the chart on the next page to see how your communication with yourself can affect your behavior, attitude, and reality.

Limiting Belief	Empowering Belief	Origin of Limiting Belief
I can't have the life I want.	I deserve to have unlimited abundance, success, prosperity, joy, and peace.	Family Community Culture Groups or Other Organizations
I'm not smart enough to….	I have available to me all the knowledge and resources I need to achieve the goals I desire.	Family Community Culture Groups or Other Organizations
Saying "NO" means I am selfish.	I set limits on activities and commitments so that I consistently practice good self-care.	Family Community Culture Groups or Other Organizations

Identifying the communication patterns you use to talk to yourself and then rewording them so they are no longer negative but positive is the first step in creating the empowering beliefs that will give you the confidence to communicate effectively with yourself and others.

Lovingly Separate From Negative Influences

On occasion, we all encounter angry, obstinate, whining people who complain, gossip, criticize, zap our energy, and leave us feeling drained.

I recently asked a client how he could separate lovingly from a situation filled with "conframa" [confusion and drama] that was sucking up every ounce of energy he had. He replied, "I don't know how I can lovingly separate."

My client expressed exactly what a lot of people think about when they hear the word "separate." Let me clarify, however, that "separate" does not mean physically abandoning a friendship, marriage, or any other situation that zaps your energy.

Separating is a way to release your emotional connection from the drama, confusion, pessimism, and other unacceptable behaviors. Distancing yourself from negative people is about demonstrating that you have clear emotional boundaries around what is acceptable to you and what's not.

Al-Anon, a support group for families, friends, and teens who are dealing with the effects of a loved one's drinking, teaches participants to set clear emotional boundaries and make rational decisions about what course of action needs to be taken. It provides a great blueprint for setting strong boundaries and making choices.

If, like my client, you wonder how to separate lovingly from negative influences, then here are a few suggestions:

- Avoid arguing with contrary, pessimistic people, who try to get attention—inappropriately meeting their emotional needs—through negative behaviors. Arguing with such people encourages attention-seeking behaviors. State your position clearly and move on.

- Set firm boundaries concerning the amount of time you will allow disruptive influences, minimizing their effect on your life.

- Be prudent in how you manage your energy resources. Limit energy-zapping interactions or you will not have enough energy left to take care of YOU.

- Don't try to change a negative person's attitude or behavior.

- Realize that a person's negative behavior is brought about by a need to be accepted, loved, and cared for. You can't coax, manipulate, or direct anyone else's attitude or frame of mind.

- When speaking to a negative person, reframe his or her statements with a positive spin or steer the conversation in a more positive direction. For example, if you say to someone "It's a lovely day" and she responds with "Yeah, but it's going to snow tomorrow," you can reframe the person's statement by saying something like, "Yes, it is supposed to snow tomorrow, but I'm going to enjoy this day while it's here."

- Maintain strong boundaries around your time, space, and energy. These are precious resources and they ought to be protected like any other prized possession.

- Refuse to participate in someone else's drama or negative attitude. Unless you're an actor, drama has no place in your life.

Maintain Good Self-Care to Keep an Emotionally Healthy Outlook

From time to time, a less than healthy emotional outlook weighs down most of us. Yet, that does not mean we have to dwell on it or accept it as our reality. When your emotional outlook is cloudy, it's important to allow the sun to shine through by taking some well-deserved time for self-care.

Many women today lead lives punctuated with "To-Do" lists, decision-making, family obligations, social and community activities, chauffeuring, appointments, and a host of other "To-Do's."

Yet, while all this "busy-ness" may give you a sense of accomplishment, purpose, validation, and acceptance, it comes with a high price.

The price you pay for all this busy-ness is foregoing regular and consistent self-care, and that takes a serious toll on your emotional and physical health.

Oprah Winfrey once said, "I don't have a weight problem—I have a self-care problem that manifests through weight."

Because Oprah is another very busy woman who neglected to take time for herself, she fell prey to heart palpitations, a thyroid condition, and weight gain.

Here are some clear indications that you may have an unhealthy emotional outlook and what you can do about it:

Worrying over things outside of your control: When you worry, you are trying to prevent those nasty little surprises that catch you off guard. Whenever those irritating thoughts pop up, write yourself a "worry list." Pick one worry from your list and devote ten to fifteen minutes to worrying about it. By designating "worry" time, you give yourself permission to ponder just how valid the worry is. For example, what's the worst that could happen if what you are worrying about comes true? Can you realistically do something to prevent it from happening? If you can't come up with a solution, or it's not within your control, is it really worth spending your energy and time worrying about it? Once the time is up, immediately engage in another activity that will keep your mind occupied.

Putting your needs on the back burner: Allowing your time and energy to be zapped leaves little time for your physical and mental health. This practice often leads to physical ailments, burnout, irritability, and an inability to take care of yourself and the people you care about. Schedule time to rejuvenate and relax so you have the energy to take good care of YOU while taking care of the other people in your life.

Build Resiliency: Resiliency is the ability to bounce back from adverse circumstances. For example, Michael J. Fox, star of the popular sitcoms of the 80's—"Family Ties" and "Spin City"—has shown remarkable resiliency since announcing he had Parkinson's disease in 1998. He stated this about his disease:

> If I let it affect me, it's gonna own everything. I don't deny it or pretend it's not there, but I don't allow it to be bigger than it is. I can't always control my body and I can't control whether or not I feel good…but I can control how clear my mind is and I can control how willing I am to step up if somebody needs me.

THE MOST IMPORTANT RELATIONSHIP

Having the emotional stamina to withstand life's setbacks not only builds resiliency and keeps you out of the role of victim, but it also helps you control the things within your power to control. You no longer have to worry about everything. Most of the things you worry about will never happen anyway so quit focusing on them.

Remember, your brain only responds to your subconscious voice—your beliefs are your reality. The good news is: You can change your reality!

Self-Validation: Change Your Beliefs. Change Your Life.

Ultimately, you have the power to make choices that affirm and support your endeavors, and you determine your response to the situations in your life.

No, you can't change how past experiences played out, but you can change the way you think about them and how those experiences influence how you feel now.

YOU have the power to do that, and you can choose to use that power to change your mindset by:

- Changing your perceptions, patterns, and behaviors

- Taking full responsibility for your actions, decisions, and choices

105

When you look to others for approval, acceptance, and validation, you give them more power than they deserve. The approval you are seeking comes from within and not from others.

Use the tips below to start validating the uniquely wonderful person you are and start creating the life you truly deserve and want:

- Place a gold star on a calendar every time you reach a milestone or achieve a goal.

- Set realistic expectations for yourself and others.

- Buy yourself a special treat just because you can and you deserve it

- Give yourself a hug at least once a day. (It is said that we need four hugs a day for optimum health. Once you hug yourself, you only have three more to go!)

- Slow down—define what is important to you and do those things regularly.

- Do away with the "all or nothing perfectionist attitude"—decide what "good enough" is for you and accept that.

- Laugh more—laughter produces happy endorphins and promotes a sense of well-being.

- Be grateful—focus on what you are grateful for. (It's the best way to curb negative thoughts.)

Every achievement, reaction, and goal you have begins with a subconscious thought. To change your behavior, you must spend time cultivating positive, uplifting, and affirming thoughts to reflect what you want most. Just like the genie metaphor, you have permission to grant yourself any wish you desire.

Sometimes you've just got to give yourself what you wish someone else would give you.

— Phil McGraw

CHAPTER 8

Creating Space for Quiet Time and Reflection

"We need quiet time to examine our lives openly and honestly...spending quiet time alone gives your mind an opportunity to renew itself and create order."

— Susan Taylor

We are consumed by "time poverty" and "busyness." In August 2010, STUDYLOGIC, a market research company specializing in response generation and online survey execution, surveyed fifteen hundred employed professionals. Westin Hotels & Resorts commissioned the survey. The study found that 64 percent of workers admitted canceling or postponing a vacation in the previous year and 33 percent of those canceling a vacation said it was due to stress at work, overwhelming responsibilities, or a lack of time to plan a vacation.

I've found that postponing vacation time leaves me feeling scattered, unproductive, and irritable. Quiet time for reflection and rest invigorates your mind, body, and spirit.

So often we're so busy "doing" that time just to "be" gets pushed to the back burner. Our time is so filled with mindless activities that we crowd out the opportunity to dream and identify the things that matter most to us.

We all need time that contributes to our well-being. That kind of time falls into two categories:

1. **Quality Time with Others.** Quality time is the time spent giving another person one's undivided attention in order to strengthen a relationship. According to the American Time Use Survey (ATUS) released by the U.S. Bureau of Labor Statistics (BLS) in 2010, Americans watch 2.8 hours of television per day. When we spend this much time in pursuit of things that give us a false sense of being (watching television, playing computer games, etc.) we forfeit spending quality time with our loved ones.

2. **Personal Quiet Time.** We all need some personal time to unwind, to be at one with ourselves, time to reflect on our daily lives, or to engage in a hobby we enjoy such as playing the piano, gardening, reading, meditating. Having our own quiet time allows us to reenergize ourselves.

Time is in short supply these days. In the book *Take Back Your Time: Fighting Overwork and Time Poverty in America* by John De Graaf, we are encouraged to organize a Take Back Your Time Day on the fourth Friday in October. Following are some other ways you can find the time you need so you can feel fulfilled and rejuvenated:

Create a sacred space: You may not have a room dedicated as your sacred space, but surely there's a corner somewhere in your home you can designate as your own. Maybe it's a corner in your bedroom or dining room or somewhere else you can spend quiet time without being disturbed.

Sometimes doing nothing in your sacred space is the best thing you can do for yourself.

I am fortunate to have a separate space off of my bedroom where I can see the sun peeking through the window early in the morning. I can hear the birds chirping and neighbors starting cars headed out to work, but none of that disturbs my sense of peace and quiet. There was a time when I felt uncomfortable with the quietness because I thought, erroneously, that I had to be doing something! But sometimes doing nothing in your sacred space is the best thing you can do for yourself.

Journal your thoughts: Writing has always been an escape for me. I have several journals where I record travel, daily musings, and milestones. In the past, my journals would often end up with some empty pages. That's because I didn't always value the quiet time I needed to journal consistently. A journal is a good

111

way to sort out your thoughts, record observations, and in some cases, come up with new insights.

Meditate: Once I discovered that meditation is simply an exercise to quiet your mind, I was able to engage in it more easily. Like a lot of people, I had visions of monks sitting for hours on end, deep in a trance-like state in order to meditate. But you can actually do it for just five minutes. For example, I learned to close my eyes and deliberately focus on noticing my breathing; even when I get distracted, having something to focus on helps me to limit distracting thoughts. For some people, a candle or other object serves the same purpose as focusing on breathing. Whatever quiet time you can lend to meditating can help you to rejuvenate and to focus throughout the rest of the day.

Personal time to meditate, journal or sit quietly for a few minutes is a perfect opportunity to rejuvenate and relax your mind, body and spirit. What will you do to create quiet time for yourself?

_____

_____

_____

_____

CHAPTER 9

Simplify and Systematize Your Life

"Simplicity is making the journey of this life with just baggage enough."

— *Author Unknown*

Despite herculean attempts to check off successfully everything I have on my To-Do list, I sometimes feel like I am trying to fit a square peg in a round hole!

According to the National Association of Professional Organizers, 60 percent of Americans feel they do not have enough time to get everything done.

I've certainly been a part of that 60 percent!

Sometimes all the busyness and things we have to do get in the way of allowing us to be the person we really are. In this chapter, we'll look at ways to get back to the basics so that our genie can shine through.

De-Clutter Your Life

A sense of balance and clarity is impossible when you are surrounded by clutter.

Do you know that a quarter of homeowners with two-car garages use their garages exclusively for storage and park in the driveway?

How did we become hostages to the jumble of odds and ends that once gave us pleasure and evoked fond memories, but are no longer meaningful?

When I finally took on the gigantic task of clearing the clutter from my basement and garage, I felt lighter, energized, and ready to tackle other tasks! Whew!

Balance and clarity is impossible when you are surrounded by clutter.

How many times did I say, "We really need to clear out some stuff from the garage," and let it be merely a passing comment? I just never got to it. So to solve the problem, I tried my best to ignore the growing mound of useless odds and ends that had taken over my space.

Finally, I could no longer tolerate it. So amongst the empty soda cans, unused boxes of (ugly) tile, stacks of old magazines, bits of broken tables, unwanted gifts, and dead electronics, I set out to simplify my life from the outside in. I can now get in and out of my car without banging the door into boxes of Christmas decorations I haven't used in many years.

I realized a long time ago that I do not work well or feel productive when there is a lot of disorder. Yet, here I was, again being slowly consumed by the clutter monster.

Look around you—is the clutter monster steadily gobbling you up?

Did you know that clutter in your surroundings directly affects how you think, work, and live?

Let's categorize what clutter may look like:

- Things you do not use or love

- Things that are untidy or disorganized

- Too many things in too small a space

- Anything unfinished

Most professional organizers focus on orderliness and systems to maintain tidy surroundings. But I want you to consider how clutter can also symbolize your state of mind.

What old beliefs about letting go are you clinging to?

When you imagine de-cluttering, what emotions do you feel? (Are you feeling a sense of loss, hurt, anxiety, or confusion?)

Do you find it difficult to make room for new thoughts, ideas, and actions?

How do you feel when clutter gets the best of you? Is it difficult for you to make changes? Does the thought of changing make you uncomfortable?

The best way to begin is with your thoughts about clutter. Change your thoughts, and change your life!

Yes, I know I'm guilty of not always practicing what I preach! I sometimes let the clutter monster come for a visit. And it's usually when my mind is filled with disorder. The times when I am thinking clearly and can be organized are the times when there seems to be less clutter around me.

When you find you're surrounded by disorganization, holding on to things long past their prime, and ignoring the clutter, give some thought to your state of mind. Are you anxious, uncomfortable, holding on to old hurts, confused, and unmotivated? If you experience any of these feelings, I'm sure you will see it reflected in your surroundings.

Don't just move things around; you must be willing to flush out the clutter monster and let go of unnecessary objects.

Take a long hard look at how clutter is affecting your surroundings and your thoughts. Start purging now and make room to attract the things you want most.

The To-Do List

Maybe you're also overwhelmed with the sheer volume of items on your To-Do list! Or, perhaps, you underestimated the time needed or fell prey to interruptions because you didn't set strong time boundaries.

With a mountain of paperwork facing you, phone calls to make, tasks/chores to be done and all the other things you want to check off your To-Do list, you're more than likely to procrastinate and shuffle mindlessly from one thing to another. And, at the end of the day, you may feel you have wasted time and accomplished little, if anything.

When I find myself stuck in a To-Do time warp, I take a power hour to stop "overwhelm" in its tracks, take a step back, re-energize, and reassess what's really important "right now."

By taking a "power hour," you can quickly get from overwhelmed, foggy, and frustrated to seeing some astonishing results while renewing your energy and gaining clarity and a sense of achievement.

Set a timer and work on just one task for an hour. Setting a time to complete one task helps you manage your time and gives you a sense of accomplishment. When the hour is up, take a ten-minute break—get something to drink or go for a short walk.

When you return, you will feel mentally and physically alert and ready to take on the next task on your list.

Use part of your ten-minute break to take several deep breaths. Breathing deeply gives you clarity, focus, and renewed energy.

If it fits into your day, take a power nap. A power nap is a good way to refresh quickly.

Researchers at NASA showed that a thirty-minute power nap increased mental alertness by approximately 40 percent! I find ten- to fifteen-minute naps refreshing.

Before you go back to your list, realign your expectations and reality. What is actually possible to accomplish within a given timeframe? Rome wasn't built in a day and you won't accomplish everything on your schedule today.

Set strong boundaries on how much time and energy you spend engaged in activities that drain you and prevent you from taking care of yourself first so you will preserve enough energy to take care of everything else on your plate.

Prioritize your To-Do list based on what's most important NOW.

If your workspace is cluttered, spend the first hour of the day clearing away all unnecessary papers, pens, etc. before you begin working on your first task. Note: This is not the time to rearrange files, read email, clean out a drawer, sort books, etc. Instead, your main goal is to clear a space where your energy and creativity can flow freely.

Develop a filing system to hold important papers and follow up items so your workspace is clear.

Focus on just one task at a time. For example, if you are working on a proposal, have only the things pertinent to the proposal on your desk.

Turn off the ringer on your phone and let calls go to voicemail so you are not interrupted. You can always check for messages when you take your next break.

Professional organizers swear by prioritization and developing systems and techniques to overcome project paralysis. Tackling one thing at a time before moving on to the next task gives you a sense of accomplishment and is inspiring. Before undertaking the next thing on your list, you might want to consider adding at least one task that you can do everyday that is enjoyable and gives you a sense of control, such as reading a chapter of an inspiring book, taking a leisurely walk, exercising, writing in your journal or painting. When you see that you've accomplished a task, you create inspiration, momentum, and the freedom to choose the things that you enjoy and to take control of your life.

Life is not measured by the number of breaths we take, but by the moments that take our breath away.

— Maya Angelou

CHAPTER 10

You Are the Captain of Your Soul

Invictus

Out of the night that covers me,
Black as the Pit from pole to pole,
I thank whatever gods may be
For my unconquerable soul.
In the fell clutch of circumstance
I have not winced nor cried aloud.
Under the bludgeoning of chance
My head is bloody, but unbowed.
Beyond this place of wrath and tears
Looms but the Horror of the shade,
And yet the menace of the years
Finds, and shall find, me unafraid.
It matters not how strait the gate,
How charged with punishments the scroll.
I am the master of my fate:
I am the captain of my soul.

— William Ernest Henley

My fifth grade teacher, Mrs. Westgate, was a literary genius, or so I thought at the ripe old age of ten. Her diction was perfect and to hear her read was a magical experience. Each week we were required to learn a poem and recite it in front of the class. I still remember one of those poems, "Invictus," to this day.

Maybe Henley didn't intend his poem to be taken quite as literally as I've taken it. But as an adult revisiting this poem, the meaning I attach to it takes on a broader significance for me.

Your Right to Choose What's Best for YOU

I am the captain (the master) of my soul. Those are powerful and empowering words!

When you're the master of your soul, you make choices and decisions that empower you and you have in place strong boundaries so that you aren't burdened by unrealistic demands on your time and energy.

Your boundaries are the foundation of every action you take or reaction you have. Setting limits on what others can do to you, or say to you, is the building block to loving the woman you see in the mirror every day.

Who do you see hidden beneath the roles you play and the titles you hold (roles and titles like mother, grandmother, daughter, sister, friend, nurse, doctor, social worker, teacher, counselor, administrative assistant, office manager, technician)? Now imagine all those roles and titles are stripped away until you see who you truly are; then make choices based on the image of your true self.

Just for a moment, I want you to close your eyes.

Picture yourself standing in front of a mirror...on your face is a mask hiding your eyes, nose, forehead, chin, and ears...all you can see is this mask. On this mask are written these words: mother, grandmother, friend, wife, partner, daughter, nurse, social worker, teacher, doctor, sister, aunt, cousin. These words entirely cover the mask. You see the words clearly.

What do you see hidden beneath the roles you play and the titles you hold?

Now imagine peeling away each of those roles... you can now see beneath the mask. You're looking at your inner core...who you really are deep down inside...you're looking at the confident, wise, authentic YOU.

You can see yourself as:

- Radiating with confidence and clarity

- Taking charge of your time, energy, and resources

- Making your desires a priority

- Expressing your values and opinions confidently wherever you go

- Making decisions that honor and affirm your brilliance

- Being "good enough"

- Successful in your chosen career

The authentic woman you're seeing in the mirror now is the very foundation on which you live your life. It's the foundation for what you will accept, do, be, give, and allow in your life.

The roles assigned to women are just a smokescreen that cloud who you really are. People might say, "She's a great partner, friend, employee," but you can't be a great anything if you don't believe you are valuable and worthwhile, and you don't stand up for what you want and deserve, and not let people walk all over you like you are a doormat.

So now, to reinforce your inner beliefs about who you really are, list five positive statements about yourself:

1. _____

2. _____

3. _____

4. _____

5. _____

Repeat your positive qualities daily until you erase the limiting mask of fear and self-doubt and discard expectations that don't confirm your authenticity.

Your Good Enough is Enough

The concept of "good enough" comes from psychiatrist and psychoanalyst John Bowlby's theory about "good enough parenting." The premise is that children can and do thrive with parental substitutes (relatives, adoptive parents, etc.) and that this mothering is good enough even when the child is deprived of a connection with his or her birth mother.

As I thought about this theory, I couldn't help but wonder when good enough is enough in other areas of our lives.

We are taught early to avoid (what is considered) failure at all cost. In our schools, we learn to strive for an "A" while anything less is considered not good enough.

What about those students who get a "C"? Have they failed?

Of course not. Their "C" is good enough and probably the best they can do at that time. We all won't be "A" students.

The underlying message is not that the grade is a failure, but rather "you" aren't good enough. That's the message we internalize and it becomes part of the program running our lives—a program filled with doubt, fear, and a deep-seated belief that we aren't good enough.

Most of us have been programmed for perfection. However, I think Mary Poppins was right when she said, "Enough is as good as a feast."

Just imagine a table filled with the finest meats, vegetables, and desserts where you can have as much as you want. You eat until you're full. Would you continue eating until you got sick, or would your stomach signal you've had enough?

Sometimes, you just have to respond to the signal that good enough is enough and let go of self-limiting expectations.

Good enough is enough.

A friend of mine often told me, "I have to clean my house," when I invited her to join me in what could have been an enjoyable, fun experience. It's nice to have your surroundings neat and clean, but at some point, good enough ought to be enough. Besides, will your guests think any less of you if they spot a lone dust bunny in the corner or a cobweb or two hanging from the corner of your ceiling? What's more important—spending quality time with the people you care about or worrying that your home won't pass the white glove test?

The notion of perfection is a limiting belief that makes you think anything less than perfect is unacceptable.

Unless you are a heart surgeon, your good enough is enough.

"Our deepest fear is not that we are inadequate. Our deepest fear is that we are powerful beyond measure. It is our light, not our darkness that most frightens us. We ask ourselves, Who am I to be brilliant, gorgeous, talented, fabulous? Actually, who are you not to be? You are a child of God. Your playing small does not serve the world. There is nothing enlightened about shrinking so that other people won't feel insecure around you. We are all meant to shine, as children do. We were born to make manifest the glory of God that is within us. It's not just in some of us; it's in everyone. And as we let our own light shine, we unconsciously give other people permission to do the same. As we are liberated from our own fear, our presence automatically liberates others."

– Marianne Williamson, *A Return to Love*

If you take the above quote to heart, you will easily realize how powerful and limiting fear can be. Ask yourself the following questions about the role of fear in your life:

- Do you minimize your accomplishments or shrink into the woodwork when it's your time to shine?

- Are you settling for less than you deserve in your personal life, career, or social connections?

- Is your personal life out of sorts?

- Are you stuck in an unfulfilling career?

- Do you spend more time focused on other people's problems than your own?

- Are you hiding your talents and brilliance by not stepping out boldly?

Fear is a natural and necessary emotion just like any other emotion.

Fear is just an unpleasant feeling of risk or danger, either real or imagined. It should serve as a motivation to escape or retreat, not as a way to keep us from pursuing our dreams.

We do a lot of things that will comfort us to avoid the feeling of fear. When we are fearful of making a mistake, we won't take risks and we lack the confidence in our unique creative brilliance to make our own choices.

Look at your life now.

What have you put off doing?

128

What do you really want?

Are you avoiding acknowledging your talents?

Every action you take will produce a result, and you get to decide what that result means. Failure is only failure if you decide it is failure.

Thomas Edison was the master of this belief. He tried more than a thousand times to invent an electric light bulb that would work. But he never saw any of his experiments as failures. Each time he did not succeed in making the light bulb work, he saw it as a stepping stone.

He realized he was one step closer because he knew what would not work and he could learn from it. He trusted that if he kept on going he would eventually achieve the desired result.

Failure is only a failure if you decide it's a failure.

Although Edison's peers ridiculed him, Edison had persistence and knew that he could not fail as long as he kept taking action.

Fear helps to keep us safe and is a built-in mechanism in humans to protect us from danger. But fear is not meant to keep us from living fulfilling lives. Rather than let fear limit us, we can choose to use it as an energetic motivator to experiencing life as an adventure.

A friend of mine said that whenever she is afraid to do something—especially speak in public—she makes certain she does it so it doesn't hold her back.

Another friend of mine (I have incredible friends) said she believes the only thing to fear is regret. This statement is not only a powerful but also a wise one.

How sad it would be one day to realize your life could have been much more gratifying and enjoyable if you had only not allowed fear to keep you from sharing your unique gifts with the world.

Following are two ways to master fear in your life so you can use it to your advantage:

Eliminate the fear with yourself and others: When you encounter people who focus on the negative, notice quickly that you also begin to focus on the negative. Begin interjecting more positive ideas into your conversations. Speak with integrity and refrain from engaging in negative conversations and meaningless activities that waste valuable time you could instead be spending developing courage and confidence.

Practice self-mastery: Strive to take control of your conversations, your actions, and your reactions. Here is where you begin to shift from a limiting mindset that eats away your authenticity. A very practical and powerful guide to living authentically can be found in *The Four Agreements: A Practical Guide to Personal Freedom* by Miguel Ruiz. Simply put, the four agreements are:

1. Be Impeccable With Your Words
2. Don't Take Anything Personally
3. Don't Make Assumptions
4. Always Do Your Best

These four agreements are a practical guide for living authentically, confidently, and in harmony with your best self.

Here are a few additional suggestions so you can shake away fear and step boldly into your magnificence:

Become an authenticity magnet: Once you commit to striving for authenticity, the next step is turning your attention to others who are authentic. Like attracts like. And when you are fully committed to authenticity, you will attract others who are focused and committed to living their best lives.

Take a risk: We all have faced challenges, obstacles, conflicts, and struggles. And we must not let these things stop us from taking risks. I'm certainly not suggesting you do anything dangerous or harmful, but carefully consider stretching yourself to do more, achieve more, and be more! Playing it safe is a direct path to regret.

Dare to be different: No one knows better than you what you want, so set your own expectations.

Trying to live up to someone else's expectations is a sure way to sabotage your authenticity.

Please yourself first: If you are busy making sure everyone else is happy and getting along, ask yourself, "How happy am I in this role"?

Re-energize regularly: When you find yourself running on the proverbial hamster wheel, stop and take time to replenish your energy so you can take care of yourself and the other people in your life.

Show up bold and confident and step into your limelight. The world is waiting for you!

Look Within to Find the Answers

The Wizard of Oz is a 1939 musical fantasy film in which Judy Garland starred as Dorothy Gale. Dorothy is swept away to a magical land when a tornado hits her home in Kansas. She then sets out on a journey to find the Wizard who she believes can help her find her way back home.

Like Dorothy and the other characters in *The Wizard of Oz*, we often search for someone or something to guide us back home.

Dorothy and the other characters all thought the Wizard would give them what they were looking for...

Dorothy dreamed of finding her way home to Kansas.

The Scarecrow believed he would be happy when he had a brain.

The Tin Man thought he would be happy if he only had a heart.

The Cowardly Lion thought he would find happiness with some courage.

The characters in *The Wizard of Oz* thought they didn't have what they needed to be happy, successful, courageous, and to live satisfying lives.

Just as a lot of us do, they were looking outside of themselves for answers. And as is most often the case, everything they needed was already within their reach.

When you can't find your true self and feel lost, you may need a gentle nudge from your inner self to remind you that you have access to everything you need to be joyful, fearless, and confident. Open yourself up to the answers that are deep within you. The more open you are to receiving the answers, the more of your authentic self will emerge. Tap into your inner genie to help get you on your way.

Remember, the only thing that kept Dorothy, the Scarecrow, the Tin Man, and the Cowardly Lion from getting what they wanted was their own thoughts. Change how you think and the solutions you desire will be evident.

List here the thoughts that keep you from finding your way back to your true self (home)?

_____

_____

_____

_____

_____

If you find it difficult to list your thoughts, ask your inner genie for the answers. She's ready to grant your wishes. Just ask her!

CHAPTER 11

Give Without Giving Up Yourself

"Don't compromise yourself. You are all you've got."

—*Janis Joplin*

You may be stuck in what I call the giving mode. If so, it's time to stop and rewrite the script that is playing in your head and take a hard look at the ways you are giving.

Giving is not the problem. It's an admirable trait to be a giver. However, it is a problem when you give up yourself for the perceived approval, acceptance, and recognition of others. Sacrificing your time, limited resources, and self-preservation will not give you the validation you are seeking. You must respect the boundaries you set for yourself. Say, "No" and mean it. Take ownership of what you can give without giving up yourself in the process.

When you take on more than what you are responsible for, giving more of yourself than is necessary, you set yourself up for long-term exhaustion, poor boundary making, lack of energy, and just being plain burnt out.

Not speaking up when you are insulted, disrespected, or treated unkindly is another form of giving up yourself.

Are you comfortable telling your family, friends, co-workers, and partners how you really feel? Or do you beat around the bush, expecting them to know what you mean and not wanting to upset anyone?

When your words are "wishy-washy" (lacking in strength, character, or purpose; ineffective; or bland), you are telling the listener that your position is weak, you are unsure, you lack confidence, and you are doubtful about what you are saying.

Telling others how you feel is also one of the most important gifts you can give, and it can make both your life and the lives of others more rewarding. When you speak up boldly and with confidence, you are saying, "I am a force to be reckoned with. I command respect, and I am worth listening to."

You don't have to be rude or insulting to get your point across. For example, when someone does something that upsets you, do you start the conversation with "You are _____," "You never _____," or "You always _____"?

If you find yourself starting conversations this way, check yourself and instead refer to the specific incident that affected you. For example, you can say, "When you did ____, I FELT ____." Just tell the person how his or her comment made YOU feel and don't try to determine what the other person meant or felt or what his or her motives were.

By now, you have a clear understanding of what keeps you struggling to strike a balance.

Now that you are aware of things you want to be, do, or have in your life, complete the following questions with one goal (target) in mind—achieving the stated goal within six weeks. Ensure the goal, when achieved, will make a BIG difference to your life. (Be specific).

What is the one big thing I want to achieve most in my life right now that would make the greatest difference?

_____

_____

_____

What action steps can I take now to achieve this ONE thing?

_____

_____

_____

Why am I ready to tackle this ONE thing now?

_____

_____

You have now identified one thing you want to achieve; you know why you want it, and you have outlined the steps to get you there.

Once you have reached your goal, answer the following questions:

Which of your beliefs have changed?

_____

_____

What "aha moment" did you have?

_____

_____

Complete this exercise often to keep on track with achieving even greater goals while creating breathing space in your busy life.

Remember, you change from the inside out.

CHAPTER 12

Set Limits on Your Time and Energy

"Every time I say 'no' to something that is not important, I am saying 'yes' to something that is."

— *Michael Hyatt*

The dictionary defines a boundary as "something that indicates a border or limit." For our purposes, we will define boundaries as the limits you establish for what you will or will not accept and the limits you set around how you want to be treated. Picture a boundary as the imaginary line you draw to define yourself and your space.

Several types of boundaries exist. We are going to focus mostly on internal boundaries because you will have better results establishing external boundaries when your internal boundaries are on a sure footing.

The first step is defining your boundaries. If you are unsure, unclear, or know you need to re-establish some boundaries, consider your responses to the following scenario:

You're standing in line at the supermarket. A friendly enough woman says hello and proceeds to touch your hair. How does that make you feel? Do you want to slap her hand away, move back, or would you be comfortable saying, "I feel uncomfortable when people I don't know touch me; please don't do that"?

If you are comfortable with the latter statement, you probably have good personal boundaries. But let's imagine you don't have good space boundaries, and instead of enforcing your boundary, you become angry and suffer in silence. How frustrating is that?

Personal Boundaries

Personal boundaries are the physical and emotional limitations you place on yourself. For example, do you

Feeling like a doormat? Are you protecting your personal boundaries?

speak up when someone invades your personal space? Do you try to avoid conflict at the expense of saying how you really feel? How well do you honor commitments to yourself? For example, if your mother asks you to take her shopping for the third time this week and you can't say, "No" without feeling guilt, your personal boundaries are in jeopardy of collapsing. If you are feeling like the proverbial doormat, then you're not protecting your personal boundaries.

Or imagine you and a friend are having an interesting conversation about the meaning of life and someone just walks up and interrupts your conversation, or joins in and starts to talk over you. How frustrating is it for you when people interrupt your conversations or talk over you?

Now, I want you to review the personal boundaries below and use the space provided to set or reestablish a boundary you want to enforce.

Time Boundary

Time is your most valuable resource. Without time boundaries, you are forever negotiating, and you usually end up doing things you would rather not do. For example, you probably know someone who is always running late, taking on just one more thing right before she needs to be somewhere. You're always punctual, but your friend is habitually late, and you tolerate her lateness without speaking up. You are exhibiting a weak time boundary by tolerating her lateness. Setting consistent, firm boundaries around your time clears the deck for you to engage in the activities you want to do rather than what someone else's timetable dictates. You've probably heard the saying, "A failure to plan on your part does **not** constitute an emergency on my part." When you allow other people to dictate your timetable, you are telling them you don't value your time.

Consider how you are spending your time and whether it infringes on things you would rather be doing. What boundary will you set around your time?

My Time Boundary is:

_____

_____

Example: I will only take my mother shopping on Tuesday mornings.

Energy Boundary

Good energy boundaries keep you from taking on tasks that drain your energy and they help you maintain the energy you need to operate at your best. When you give, give, give, do, do, and do more, your energy gets depleted and you turn into the Energizer Bunny—going, going, going....How much of your energy can you use filling requests, completing tasks, fulfilling commitments, etc. before you feel frustrated and drained? What boundary will you set to protect your energy?

My Energy Boundary is:

_____

_____

Example: I will only agree to help with the church bake sale every other month.

Money Boundary

Like time, money is another of your precious commodities. How do you spend money? Is it indiscriminately so that you struggle to make ends meet? Or do you set limits on your spending and save regularly?

Protecting your finances is not only good financial management; it also helps you to set boundaries for other areas of your life. Placing limits around what is acceptable to you and what's not helps define who you are, what you're all about, and what you will and won't accept. When you can set boundaries around your finances, you're in a better position to set other boundaries. What boundary do you have around money?

My Money Boundary is:

_____

_____

Example: I will limit eating out to one night a week.

Relationship Boundary

The limits you set in your personal relationships ensure that they thrive, not just survive. Whenever you compromise your personal boundaries, you're sending the message that your values and desires are not important. You get to set the rules in any relationship—how you will be treated, what's acceptable and what's not, what you will tolerate and what you will not. What relationship boundary will you establish in your family, your intimate relationships, or your workplace?

My Relationship Boundary is:

Family:

_____

_____

Example: I will not cook all the meals and then also do the dishes.

Intimate Relationship:

_____

_____

Example: I will not tolerate being in a relationship where my partner puts his friends before me.

Workplace:

_____

_____

Example: I will not work on Sundays because my family time is more important.

Self-Esteem Boundary

Self-esteem is a combination of internal confidence, outer achievements, and understanding yourself.

The word "esteem" comes from a Latin word that means "to estimate." Self-esteem is your estimate of yourself or the image you have of yourself. Self-esteem and self-confidence are often used interchangeably, but they mean different things. Self-confidence has to do with how you view your ability to achieve or manage things. Your self-esteem determines how good you feel about yourself and the image you project to the world. For example, if you are fearful about approaching others, you avoid doing things that you really want to do, you do things that just don't feel right to please others, or you often think that others can do things better than you, then your self-esteem boundaries may be weak.

My Self-Esteem Boundary is:

_____

_____

Example: I will not offer to help people who criticize my efforts.

145

Note: You may need to set several self-esteem boundaries. Think of any unacceptable behaviors you have tolerated in the past or an unacceptable behavior you are tolerating now and how you will address it. List it here:

_____

_____

_____

_____

Example: I will assertively express my opinions and wishes.

Learning What We Can and Cannot Control

Setting boundaries allows us to have control over things that may seem out-of-control in our lives. However, there is so much in life we have little or no control over. You can't control the weather or the sun rising or setting, but the good news is there are many other things you absolutely CAN control, although how to control them may not always be obvious. Here are some of them:

Let Go of Expectations. Let go of the notion that you can change another person, his or her actions, or non-actions. Your moral compass may not be the same as someone else's. When you let go of the expectations you have of others, you will no longer allow anyone to yank your chain, causing knee-jerk reactions fraught with havoc, frustration, and anxiety. Instead, you can have more control over your own life. It opens up your mind to focus on your own life and gives you more time to focus on what truly matters to YOU.

Know the Difference Between Self-Confidence and Controlling. Confidence means you believe in your ability to set consistent boundaries, priorities, and realistic expectations for yourself and others. To control means you wish to manage the actions of others and/or the outcome of things around you. Remember, the only person you have any control over is YOU. As your confidence level grows, you will be able to let go of the outcomes of things you have no control over.

Coach People on How You Want to be Treated. A crucial step in having more control over your life is the ability to teach others how you wish to be treated. You don't have control over their actions; however, you do have control over how you allow others to treat you. If you find yourself constantly stressed by the things you let other people bring into your life, you may want to begin asking yourself, "Is it worth having these people or things in my life any longer, or what boundaries can I set that will protect me from negativity, demands, and commitments?"

Make yourself a priority and you will find that others will treat you with the respect you deserve. Remember, no one can walk over you unless you willingly lie down.

Keep these tips in mind as you set personal boundaries to make sure you stay focused and in control of YOU!

CHAPTER 13

Stop the Merry-Go-Round!
I Want to Get Off

"Don't buy into the notion that it is selfish to think of yourself first."

— *Author Unknown*

L ike most women, I find myself occasionally wearing too many hats—and you know from earlier how I feel about wearing hats. But, when I allow myself the time to alter my thinking and set boundaries and priorities, even when my plate is running over, I realize I still have the power to make choices about the things I want to do and include in my life.

You can either choose to stay mired in "overwhelm" or change the way you are thinking. When you try to squeeze in one more task, take on one more responsibility, and try to be all things to all people, you open yourself up to burn-out, exhaustion, frustration, resentment, anger, anxiety, and disappointment.

But, when you change the way you think by setting clear, firm boundaries, you are setting limits that will protect you from taking on and tolerating more than you want. You can find a little more energy, feel less stressed, and be able to step back, analyze the situation, and take a course of action that makes what is important to you a priority.

How Do You Get Off the Merry-Go-Round?

Are you taking on more and more responsibilities and feeling overwhelmed and guilty if you don't get everything done?

Do you feel like you are on a perpetual hamster wheel moving too fast to get off?

If so, you can start to slow down by using the exercise below:

> *Taking care of yourself first is not selfish.*

Make sure the things you want to do for yourself are under the "Do or Die" column. The reason you put yourself under the Do or Die column is because **YOU** are that important! If you don't take care of yourself first, you won't have the energy to take care of anyone else.

Push aside or eliminate the things that "would be nice," but are not critical.

Prioritize the things under "I can do later..." into either another day or week. The important thing is to recognize you don't have to do it now. You may even be able to push some things aside for a month or more.

Recognize that not everything has to be a priority. Remember, a priority is anything that is important to YOU!

Do or Die	Would be nice if I got it done but not critical	I can do this later or another day

This list is not meant to take the place of tasks you need to accomplish to maintain your home or employment. It is your personal survival To-Do list. As I said earlier, for the same reason you are told to put on your oxygen mask first if there is an emergency on a flight, you must nurture and take good care of yourself first so you are capable of taking care of others.

Don't buy into the notion that it is selfish to think of yourself first.

When you give and give and do more and more, you rob yourself of precious energy that could better be used replenishing yourself.

And when you feel rested, joyful, confident, and re-energized, you open the door to look at all the other tasks before you as joys rather than drudgery.

Here are some suggestions that will help you put things in perspective:

- **Make a commitment to carve out self-time daily**. Start small with something you enjoy and build on that. Take five- or ten-minutes just to sit quietly and relax.

- **Relax, Refocus.** Enjoy a soothing cup of tea. Tea is a natural relaxant, and while sipping tea, you can begin to refocus. Maybe tea or coffee isn't your beverage of choice. Another soothing drink may be for you. It doesn't matter if you have something to drink or not. The important thing is to commit to carving out relaxing self-time on a daily basis.

- **Let go of the guilt.** Guilt is the result of a faulty sense of responsibility. It's often associated with anxiety and sometimes depression. Do what you can and then step back and accept the choices you have made.

- **Don't stress over what others are doing or not doing.** You have no control over others' actions. Keep in mind that you can only be responsible for the things that are your responsibility.

- **Prioritize.** For the most part, women tend to prioritize according to the needs of others—not themselves. Putting your needs first is not a selfish act, but rather a selfless one. Remember the oxygen mask on the plane. You have to survive first before you can think of saving someone else.

- **Allow friends to support and encourage you.** Most of us can easily and willingly grumble to friends about how busy we are and how little time we have for ourselves. Having someone to complain to is not support. Surround yourself with people who offer suggestions, give of themselves if need be, and encourage and uplift you.

- **Make an appointment with YOU.** When you are keeping track of all the other appointments and To-Do lists on your schedule, put an appointment for YOU in your planner or calendar.

- **Pamper yourself.** Schedule a massage, manicure/pedicure, hair appointment, or treat yourself to lunch at your favorite restaurant.

- **Start small.** Remember, your life is not a marathon. Multitasking is like running a marathon without putting in the training to be successful.

- **Take baby steps.** Build upon these steps until they become a habit and you automatically take time for yourself.

Someday is NOW

I don't buy lottery tickets, but if I did, I would be among the many who invest in the fallacy that "someday" I'll become the next multi-millionaire. A lot of us are living our lives waiting to hit the illusive jackpot. And for some of us, the jackpot is—"when I get settled" (whatever that means), "after I pay off some debt," "as soon as I can find time," "when the last child is off to college," and other far-off reward thinking.

Why not enjoy as much of the journey as possible now and not put off joy today for that magical reward when you arrive at some illusive destination?

What have you missed by spending a big portion of your life waiting…and missing out on some delicious opportunities to savor the moment?

As a young girl, I can remember my grandmother waiting...saving gifts and other belongings for some vague special occasion. As I noticed more and more of my grandmother's "some days," I made a promise to myself that I would not wait to enjoy life or any of my posses-sions. No calendar I know of has "some day" as an option.

Don't wait for "some day" to enjoy life!

I didn't have a voice for it then, but at that point, I must have decided that I would enjoy the abundance that came my way each day. So I use the "good" crystal for a cold drink of water, drink tea from an antique cup and saucer when I want to, serve hamburgers on the "good" china midweek, and wear that new outfit as soon as I can.

Why would I wait for a holiday or other special time to take joy in the abundance all around me?

Why would you want to delay enjoying the things that have been provided for your pleasure when you can delight in them today?

One thing stopping many of us from enjoying our journey is a strong feeling of unworthiness and the deep-seated belief that we're not good enough or deserving enough of the pleasures we so freely give to others.

The feeling that we don't deserve the good things in life hinders our enjoyment of the very things that are here specifically for our benefit and pleasure.

If you have been "waiting," take a look around you.

What are you waiting for?

Here are a few simple ways to stop waiting and enjoy the good things in life:

- Reach high up on that top shelf and take down a crystal glass. (I bet your orange juice will taste better in it.)

- For dinner tonight, use your best dishes. (You can still use them for special occasions.)

- Use the "good" linen you've been saving for guests. You deserve to enjoy it too!

- Take the tags off the outfit you bought six months ago and have been waiting for a special occasion to wear. Make tomorrow your special occasion to wear it.

In the meantime, if you bought a lottery ticket, good luck!

Pretty is as Pretty Does

I often used to hear my grandmother say, "Pretty is as pretty does" whenever someone complimented one of her grandchildren on his or her looks or accomplishments.

It was one of those sayings I heard often, but usually dismissed as another message delivered in a riddle. I never really gave much thought to what it meant until recently.

As I waited in a line at the supermarket (practicing patience), I overheard a well-dressed, attractive young woman say to someone in a rather nasty tone, "What the *%&*^ are you looking at?" And, immediately I was transported back to my childhood and hearing my grandmother's voice, "Pretty is as pretty does."

No matter how well-dressed, articulate, or well-connected you are, if you are not pretty on the inside, you present your ugly side to the world—just like the woman I overheard spouting ugliness. It's not what's on the outside that counts, but what's on the inside. That's what my grandmother meant by pretty is as pretty does.

Here are some things you can keep in your tool-box so you can be pretty inside and out.

- **Hammer:** Use your hammer to drive away negative thoughts, feelings, and irritability. When you are stressed, you are prone to irritability and insensitive comments. Learn ways to reduce stress so you aren't constantly in a foul mood.

MASTER THE GENIE WITHIN

- **Nails**: Each nail in your toolbox represents one of your personal boundaries. Develop strong personal boundaries to stay in touch with your emotions, preserve your energy, and protect your precious time.

- **Flashlight:** Your smile is your bright light. Let it guide you wherever you go. Each day when you are getting dressed to go out into the world, commit to smiling at everyone you meet. It will immediately brighten your day. No matter what you're going through, it doesn't help to dwell in negativity. Put on your smiley face.

- **Gloves:** Wear gloves so you can gently massage your bruised feelings and protect yourself from negativity. Memorize a positive affirmation to uplift you and keep you motivated. Example: I radiate confidence, grace, and happiness wherever I go.

We all have days that can feel overwhelming, overscheduled, and stressed. But it helps if you have some things in your mental toolbox to keep you uplifted, focused, and positive.

CHAPTER 14

Communication Influences How Well You Are Perceived

"To effectively communicate, we must realize that we are all different in the way we perceive the world and use this understanding as a guide to our communication with others."

— *Anthony Robbins*

Many people have said, "You have two ears and one mouth for a reason. Therefore, you should listen twice as much as you speak." In relation to people skills, this means that while the other person is talking, give him or her your undivided attention. Don't get caught in the trap of thinking about what you're going to say next, what will happen later that day, or any of the other tangents where the mind can wander. Stay focused, absorb the information given, and find a way to follow up with a question relevant to the subject.

Good communication skills include an awareness of how the receiver might be interpreting your message as well as how you send the message.

Part of being a good listener is to:

- Ask questions for clarification

- Give constructive feedback

- Use tact in a non-argumentative manner

- Use good body language including posture and eye contact

- Respect personal space

- Be acutely aware of cultural differences

- Offer genuine praise when appropriate

- Use humor if the situation warrants it

The online dictionary, www.dictionary.com, defines communication as: "the imparting of thoughts, opinions, or information by speech, writing, or signs or the exchange of information, ideas, or feelings."

There are verbal means of using language and there are nonverbal means, such as body language, sign language, and eye contact, or through media, e.g., pictures, graphics, sound, and writing.

Successful communication requires a vast repertoire of skills in intrapersonal and interpersonal processing—listening, observing, speaking, questioning, analyzing, and evaluating. Use of these processes is developmental and transfers to all areas of life: home, school, community, work, and beyond.

It is through communication that collaboration and cooperation occur.

I recently called a customer service line and spoke to someone on the phone who mumbled and practically whispered her words. I soon became inattentive, and after asking her to repeat what she said several times, I gave up and said I would have to call back at a more convenient time. I was really hoping I would get someone different the next time I called.

Here are some ways to communicate so you'll be heard every time:

- Speak in a strong, clear voice. A strong, clear voice commands attention and respect. A soft, whiny voice may be perceived as insecure, weak, and ineffective. If people constantly say "Huh," or "Say that again," you're probably mumbling. Take time to pronounce every word clearly.

- Speak deliberately and slow down, but not so slow as to have people finish your sentences because it's taking you so long to verbalize your thoughts. When you speak really fast, you're perceived as someone who is nervous and unsure of herself.

For further help, join a Toastmasters group. (Visit www.toastmasters.org to find one near you.) These groups are supportive, encouraging, and give you a platform to practice your communication skills, even if you don't plan to become a professional speaker.

Use Words with Care

Have you ever spoken words that landed you in trouble? Or maybe you said something that warranted an apology.

You may have heard that familiar saying, "Sticks and stones may break my bones, but words can never hurt me," or "They're just words." However, words are actually like dynamite so you need to use them with care.

Recent research shows that words have strong emotional, physical, and spiritual effects. Many relationships have been damaged by careless words; wars have started and ended by the use of certain words. The words you use are much more powerful than you realize. They have the power to:

- Wound or heal

- Discourage or encourage

- Tear down or build up

I don't just mean the words you speak to other people. Pay attention to the words you speak to yourself...

- What words or phrases do you habitually say to yourself?

- What words do you consistently use to describe yourself?

If you use disparaging words about yourself ("I'm too fat," "too short/tall") or constantly use limiting words like "can't," "have to," and "should," you are engaging in self-sabotage and essentially giving away your power to someone else.

You are allowing someone else's standards and expectations to define you, and you are not taking responsibility for what you want and feel.

It may be that you have chosen to take on certain tasks and responsibilities because, subconsciously, you are looking to others for approval, acceptance, or recognition.

Or, your inner and outer beliefs are out of sync and you lack clarity and healthy boundaries to assert your own personal power. Ask yourself these questions:

- How will I tolerate my decision?

- Based on what I want, how could I have made a different choice?

- What is the worst thing that could happen if I made a choice to/not to do this?

Remember, you always have a choice—you make a choice even when you think you're not making a choice, because you have chosen not to make a choice.

For example, when you say you have to go to work, that's not true; you don't *have* to go to work. You choose to go to work because you don't want to experience the consequences of not going to work—lack of food, clothing, and shelter, and a sense of accomplishment.

When you say you "have to" do something, you are taking on the role of victim and making yourself feel powerless. And when you feel powerless, you react with anger, frustration, and negative, self-defeating statements.

Do you "have to" or do you "choose to?" Are your words weak and are the underlying thoughts negative or self-defeating? What message about yourself are you sending to others when you use such weak words?

You cannot predict what others think, but you do have control of your thoughts, actions, and responses. In the next few days, pay close attention to how you respond to others—how often do you use "can't," "have to," or "should," and when do you say, "Yes" when you want to say, "No"? This self-monitoring will give you a clear indication of your level of empowerment. Choose your words carefully. Use empowering words.

Make sure your statements are focused on what you want without censoring yourself to accommodate someone else.

Be careful of what you allow into your mindset. It determines whether or not you are successful, confident, courageous, and empowered. Use the following exercise to make yourself aware of how often you are using disempowering phrases. Awareness is a key part of self-fulfillment.

For the next week every time you use a disempowering phrase (*I have to, I can't, I should, etc.*), I want you to place a quarter in a container. At the end of the week, see how many quarters you have accumulated and you will have an idea of just how often you use disempowering phrases. I trust you, so this is strictly on the honor system. Use any funds you accumulate to add to your savings account or donate to a worthy charity!

Empowering Phrases

As you are doing this exercise, catch yourself when you speak a disempowering phrase by replacing it with an empowering one. Here are some examples of empowering phrases:

- I choose to…
- I choose not to…
- I decided to…
- I decided not to…

- I will…

- I won't…

Use Affirmations to Manifest Prosperity

Affirmations are another form of communicating with yourself. Affirmations are the positive messages you send to your subconscious mind to replace negative, limiting, scarcity-filled messages with new empowering positive messages.

Let's look at the issue of prosperity as an example of how affirmations can help you. It seems like every time you pick up the newspaper or listen to the news, there's a dire economic forecast. Soon all the talk of economic disaster filters into your subconscious to form false beliefs about what is possible for your life. What thoughts are you allowing to roam freely in your mind about how prosperous you can be? When you think of prosperity, do you immediately think of money? Do you worry you won't have enough for retirement or you won't be able to pay your bills?

Having a scarcity mindset only attracts more of the same circumstances. One simple way to curtail this line of thinking is to use affirmations.

However, it's important that the affirmations you send to your subconscious are believable or they won't be effective. If I asked you to repeat "I am rich," how effective would that be? Did you unexpectedly receive a large inheritance from a long-forgotten relative or win the lottery? If you don't believe the affirmation is true, neither will your subconscious mind! Affirmations must be put into words in a way that your subconscious mind won't resist.

For example, the affirmation, "I am rich" can be reframed in a way that is more believable, such as: "I am open to becoming more prosperous every day." This statement is not only more believable, but it also creates a feeling of control and opens your mind to unlimited possibilities.

Affirmations are the positive messages you send to your subconscious mind.

Your mind won't reject this affirmation because you are declaring you can imagine the possibility of it happening.

Here are a few affirmations to get you started:

- I am willing, ready, and available to more good than I have ever experienced or imagined in my life.

- I use my thoughts and emotions to attract abundance effortlessly.

- I am open to the flow of great abundance in all areas of my life.

- I always have more than enough of everything I need.

- I create a better life one positive thought at a time.

- My day is filled with limitless potential in joy, abundance, and love.

- Today I embrace simplicity, peace, and solace.

- I expand my awareness of the hidden potential in each experience.

The more effort you put into developing and affirming a prosperity mindset, the more prosperity, positivity, and abundance you will attract into your life.

A Vision Board to Create the Life You Want

Another tool to attract what you desire most into your life is a vision board. We all have visions, but how many of our visions become a reality? One simple tool to manifest your vision is a vision board. A vision board is simply a collection of vivid images, inspiring quotes, and/or positive affirmations that represent your deepest desires.

My first introduction to vision boards was when I read *The Secret*. Like a lot of people, I was under the false impression that all I needed to do was collect some pictures and quotes, put them up where I could see them every day, and I would get what I wanted.

Wrong!

Your vision board is much more than just a hodgepodge collection of images. An important piece that is often overlooked is the "feelings" you attach to the images.

You may be holding a vision of a new car, house, or job, but if you don't experience the feeling of sitting in your dream car, walking through the door of your new house, or feeling yourself working at the job you love, all the pictures in the world won't manifest your vision.

To make your vision board even more effective, try adding affirmations.

For example, if your dream is to have more family time, you could add an affirmation to a picture of you and your family engaged in a fun activity that says, "I am enjoying spending quality time with my family." If it's a new car you're dreaming of, paste a picture of yourself next to the car and add the affirmation: "I love driving my red sports car."

Without feeling the emotions, your pictures are just pictures.

If you're ready to create your vision board, here are the steps to get you started:

1. Assemble the necessary supplies and select from various options to make the Vision Board:

a) **8-1/2 x 11 card stock.** Some experts say each area of your life should have its own space. For example, one for family, career, health, prosperity, travel, etc. This division may sound a little daunting at first, but it can also serve as a means to narrow down your focus. Use one 8-1/2 x 11 card for each area.

b) **20 x 30 card stock.** Instead of the smaller card stock, if you have the wall space for it, you may prefer the 20 x 30 or similar size. If you prefer having everything where you can see it in one place, the larger size may be a better choice. Both the larger and smaller sizes can easily be found at office supply stores.

c) **Computer-Generated Board.** For some a computer-generated board works best. Several good choices are online if this is your preference.

d) **Artist Tablet.** If you want portability, an artist tablet may work better for you.

e) **Push pins, glue, or tape** to secure your images to the poster board.

2. Search through magazines, brochures, circulars, and the Internet for pictures depicting exactly what you want to attract.

3. Once you have an assortment of images, cut them out and pin or post them on a piece of poster board.

4. Place your vision board in a prominent place where you can look at it every day and experience the emotion of that image. It's important to feel the emotions so your images will become real in your mind.

Take Action

Just because you have created a vision board and experienced the emotions doesn't mean your dream will materialize. You must take action and not depend on luck. Luck is what happens when you are prepared for the opportunity.

Creating a vision board without experiencing the emotions attached to the images, being prepared to take action, and believing is like sitting around counting raindrops.

You must first believe you deserve your dream, imagine yourself in it, and feel the emotions of having what you desire. It won't happen if you just park yourself in front of your vision board wishing and hoping.

Take action now!

*What lies behind us and
what lies before us are
tiny matters compared to
what lies within us.*

— Ralph Waldo Emerson

CHAPTER 15

CELEBRATE YOU!

"Everything is created from moment to moment, always new. Like fireworks, this universe is a celebration and you are the spectator contemplating the eternal Fourth of July of your absolute splendor."

— *Lucille Francis*

Congratulations are in order! You have now finished this book! That means you have something to celebrate. And you don't have to wait for a designated time to do it.

How often have you worked hard to accomplish something in your life only to let the accomplishment or event pass by with hardly a notice?

Women may be more susceptible to ignoring the importance of rewarding themselves for a job well done because traditionally, with the exception of Mother's Day, women haven't celebrated accomplishments in the home, such as getting children to graduate from school, maintaining an orderly and clean household, or throwing a stellar dinner party.

Men, on the other hand, have always been encouraged to celebrate their achievements—promotions, fatherhood, and sporting events—with the ritual of cigars, spirits, and buddies.

Although times have changed and many women are out there in the world making a difference, we still need to remind ourselves to stop, breathe, and pat ourselves on the back.

So what can we do to make sure we celebrate our success?

To celebrate means to have fun, observe, rejoice, or commemorate. Remember, there's no date on the calendar that says "some day."

If you've completed a class, lost weight, or kept a commitment to yourself, you have something to celebrate—NOW.

What things have you accomplished but let pass by without taking the time to notice and celebrate?

Can you think of a way to reward yourself for your accomplishments?

And no, rewarding yourself for the good things you do is not being self-indulgent or conceited. Simply put, you celebrate YOU by acknowledging your successes no matter how small you think they are.

If you're not in the habit of doing things to Celebrate YOU, then the following can serve as a guide:

- Buy a bouquet of flowers for yourself. This is one of my favorites, and you can do this not just to celebrate but anytime you need a lift.

- Delight in a day of pampering. Give someone a chance to give to you instead of the other way around. If you usually do your own hair or nails, schedule an appointment at a salon.

- Toot your own horn. Plan a milestone birthday party just the way you want it. You don't have to wait for a birthday. Why not plan a Tuesday party and celebrate all the good things that have happened in your life on a Tuesday or a particular date in a month.

- Treat yourself to a fun activity that you rarely have time to do.

- Indulge in some deliciously sinful dessert or some other treat you usually pass on. Even while watching the calories, you can treat yourself in moderation.

- Establish and enforce a boundary. Give yourself a high five and celebrate with a friend who supports you.

- Have you completed a project for work or home? Buy a nice plant for yourself or treat yourself to some fun activity.

- Did you go to the gym every day all week? Treat yourself to a new piece of workout clothing or some new music for your iPod or MP3 player.

- Did you get your first article published? Plan a party and invite friends who will encourage you and celebrate your accomplishment. Yes, toot your own horn!

- Lost that last ten pounds! Take a vacation day and pamper yourself by doing something you enjoy that makes you feel contented.

List here some of your accomplishments you can start celebrating today:

_____

_____

_____

_____

_____

_____

It's never too late to celebrate your accomplishments. Think back and find a way to reward yourself for what you have already done. Remember, you are not being indulgent or conceited—you are acknowledging your successes and thanking the universe. By celebrating your accomplishments, you send notice to the universe that you are ready to attract even more wins.

Many people complain that time passes too quickly or there is not enough time to get everything done. We all have the same twenty-four hours or 1,440 minutes per day. You can't change that, but you can create breathing space in your hectic life by slowing down, relishing each moment, and celebrating YOU and your accomplishments.

I'm sure you can think of at least one or more accomplishments that you can celebrate. List them here and how you will celebrate your achievements.

_____

_____

_____

_____

_____

_____

_____

Dreams are renewable.
No matter what our age
or condition, there are
still untapped possibilities
within us and new beauty
waiting to be born.

— Dr. Dale Turner

Afterword

"If you believe you can, you probably can. If you believe you won't, you most assuredly won't. Belief is the ignition switch that gets you off the launching pad."

— Denis Waitley

No matter what belief you hold about who you are or what you are capable of doing, you have a dream or vision for your life. We all have dreams. Our dreams are a combination of our beliefs, experiences, and deepest desires. It all depends on what you believe to be true about yourself.

My hope for you after you've read this book, is that you allow those dreams to emerge by revealing the real you.

The limiting, false beliefs we hold about ourselves are like powerful swords that can cut through our confidence, self-worth, and self-esteem as sharply as a razor blade cuts through flesh.

When you change what you believe about yourself and your abilities, you unleash the genie within who grants your wish to be the courageous, confident, and clear thinking woman you were meant to be.

A joyful, confident, and purposeful life is not an option—it's your birthright. It's in your unique DNA (Divinely Natural Attributes).

Uncover, Embrace, and Celebrate the Genie Within—the True You!

List any observations or questions that have come up for you while reading this book:

_____

_____

_____

_____

_____

_____

_____

_____

_____

Use the contact form at
www.coachforyourdreams.com
to ask any questions you have.
I'll respond promptly.

181

Take a walk with a turtle.
Behold the world in pause.

— Bruce Feiler

Recommended Reading

Byrne, Rhonda. *The Secret*. New York: Atria Books, 2006.

Byron, Katie with Stephen Mitchell. *Loving What Is: Four Questions That Can Change Your Life*. New York: Three Rivers Press, 2002.

DeAngeles, Barbara. *Confidence: Finding It and Living It*. Carlsbad, CA: Hay House, 1998.

De Graaf, John. *Take Back Your Time: Fighting Overwork and Time Poverty in America*. San Francisco, CA: Berrett-Koehler, 2003.

Emmons, Robert A. *Thanks: How the New Science of Gratitude Can Make You Happier*. New York: Houghton Mifflin, 2007.

Hendrix, Harville. *Getting the Love You Want: A Guide for Couples, 20th Anniversary Edition*. 1988. New York: Henry Holt, 2008.

Hicks, Jerry and Esther. *Ask and It Is Given: Learning How to Manifest Your Desires.* Carlsbad, CA: Hay House, 2005.

Lerner, Harriet. *The Dance of Anger: A Woman's Guide to Changing the Patterns of Intimate Relationships.* 1985. New York: Quill, 2011.

Richardson, Brenda and Brenda Wade. *What Mama Couldn't Tell Us About Love: Healing the Emotional Legacy of Racism by Celebrating Our Light.* New York: HarperCollins, 2010.

Ruiz, Miguel. *The Four Agreements: A Practical Guide to Personal Freedom, A Toltec Wisdom Book.* San Rafael, CA: Amber-Allen Publishing, 1997.

Williamson, Marianne. *A Return to Love: Reflections on the Principles of "A Course in Miracles."* 1993. New York: HarperCollins, 1996.

About the Author

Affectionately known as the Self-Care Genie, Gladys Anderson holds a Master's Degree in Counseling Psychology and is a licensed marriage and family therapist and personal life coach.

Since 1997, she has had the honor to counsel and coach hundreds of couples and individuals through their pain, joy, heartaches, and struggles.

Gladys recognizes that a lot of women, despite years of formal education and professional status, still struggle to say YES to showing up in the world as their true selves.

Soon Gladys realized a lot of women she coached still struggled to give themselves permission to say "No" even when they felt over-committed, overwhelmed, and overlooked. She then became fiercely committed to teaching busy, overwhelmed women to take time for self-care. Today, she teaches women how to recognize and access The Genie Within, while making affirming choices about what they are willing to do, be, and give to reach a place of calmness, empowerment, and clarity so they can live their unique and best lives.

Besides being the author of *Master the Genie Within*, Gladys has written an e-book, *Just Say No!* and numerous self-help articles. She regularly conducts workshops on boundary setting, empowerment, confidence-building, relationships, self-control, stress-management, gratitude, life balance, communications, and other topics that help women slow down, jump off the hamster wheel, and take charge of their lives.

In her spare time, Gladys loves to travel and have new experiences. She is an amateur genealogist, avid reader, loves "techy" stuff, jazz, and enjoys reading mystery novels.

Visit Gladys online at:
www.CoachforYourDreams.com

www.ingramcontent.com/pod-product-compliance
Lightning Source LLC
LaVergne TN
LVHW051520080426
835509LV00017B/2135